The Science of Effect Communication

Improve Your Social Skills and Small Talk, Develop Charisma and Learn How to Talk to Anyone

Positive Psychology Coaching Series

Copyright © 2017 by Ian Tuhovsky

Author's blog: www.mindfulnessforsuccess.com
Author's Amazon profile: amazon.com/author/iantuhovsky
Instagram profile: https://instagram.com/mindfulnessforsuccess

Important
The book is not intended to provide medical advice or to take the place of medical advice and treatment from your personal physician. Readers are advised to consult their own doctors or other qualified health professionals regarding the treatment of medical conditions. The author shall not be held liable or responsible for any misunderstanding or misuse of the information contained in this book. The information is not indeed to diagnose, treat or cure any disease.
It's important to remember that the author of this book is not a doctor/therapist/medical professional. Only opinions based upon his own personal experiences or research are cited. The author does not offer medical advice or prescribe any treatments. For any health or medical issues – you should be talking to your doctor first.

Please be aware that every e-book and "short read" I publish is truly written by me, with thoroughly researched content 100% of the time. Unfortunately, there's a huge number of low quality, cheaply outsourced spam titles on Kindle non-fiction market these days, created by various Internet marketing companies. **I don't tolerate these books. I want to provide you with high quality, so** if you think that one of my books/short reads can be improved in some way, please contact me at:

contact@mindfulnessforsuccess.com

I will be very happy to hear from you, because you are who I write my books for!

Introduction: Why Outstanding Conversation Skills Will Change Your Life

Wherever you go, whoever you are, and whatever you want to achieve in life, your success comes down to your communication skills. It's a simple fact that the best communicators get the highest grades, the best jobs, and the most attractive partners. They are the people who light up a room just by walking through the door. Everyone wants to make friends with them, many envy them, and most of us long to know their secrets. **Thanks to this book, you'll discover exactly what they do that draws others to their presence.** It may look like magic, but you can learn how to use their strategies for yourself!

In my previous book on this topic, I shared the very best methods, tips, and strategies that anyone can use to develop their communication skills. I'm proud to say that it has already helped people of many ages and backgrounds. The positive feedback I've received has been truly humbling. However, I realized that there was room for a second book – a volume written to help people develop their conversation skills.

In this guide, I'm going to show you how to talk to anyone about anything, and overcome social awkwardness. You'll also learn how to avoid feeling like an outsider in a group situation. Don't worry if you haven't read my previous book, as this guide works as a stand-alone volume. On the other hand, I'd highly recommend that you read both. That way, as long as you are willing to put what I teach into practice, you're guaranteed to become an excellent all-around communicator.

I'm not going to sugarcoat it – improving your conversation skills is hard work. It involves breaking the habits of a lifetime, and taking a few risks along the way. But when you consider what you have to gain, it becomes a no-brainer – you can't afford to let any poor conversation skills you may have become your biggest liability. There are so many benefits you stand to gain:

1. Enhanced Career Prospects

Think about the processes you have to go through in order to secure a job, succeed at your day-to-day tasks, build rapport with your colleagues, and sprint up the career ladder. At every stage, from the initial interview to your first speech as a member of the board, your social skills need to be outstanding. If you can't talk to your colleagues, you won't be able to collaborate on projects. If you can't talk to your boss about any problems that you are facing at work, you will gain a reputation as a poor communicator. You get the point – you absolutely need to understand how to hold conversations with anyone and everyone if you are to land that dream job.

2. Better Business Relationships

Conversation is one of the pillars of great business relationships. If you've ever spoken to an extremely dull person at a conference, you'll know just how much of a barrier poor communication can be. You can be among the best in your field, but if you bore everyone you meet, you are unlikely to forge profitable, mutually beneficial deals and alliances.

3. Better Family Relationships

How many of us have tired ourselves out trying to make our parents and siblings understand us? That would be most people, right? Contrary to what the media would have us believe, most family relationships aren't naturally easy, and many actually require a lot of work. Only when you have mastered the art of conflict resolution, know how to share your views without irritating others, and understand when you need to bite your tongue when necessary can you hope to build respectful, loving family relationships.

4. Better Romantic Relationships

Along with my employment problems, this was one of my key motivators when it came to reading up on communication skills. I had a couple of girlfriends in high school and college but, for the most part, I was not a success with women. For years, I couldn't figure out where I was going wrong. When I went on a date, I would try to be warm, witty, and interesting. It took a long time to work out that the secret to great conversation is actually to focus on the other person. Still, better late than never! These days, I like to think I'm doing much better on the romance front. Whether you are a man or a woman, whether your relationship is casual or something more serious, you can look forward to fewer fights and happier times together when you improve your communication skills.

5. Improved Self-Esteem

When you enjoy success in your career, family life, and personal relationships, what's the inevitable outcome? Better self-esteem, of course. There is little so frustrating in life as the feeling you get when you aren't living up to your potential. **Have you ever had the feeling that if you had only said the right thing at the right time, your life would have taken a turn for the better?** When you've finished this book, you'll never again have to wonder about those "what-ifs." The friendships and business relationships you forge will also serve to boost your self-esteem. We are social beings, and we thrive when we are surrounded by people that make us feel accepted and content. In turn, this helps us improve our social skills still further.

Why am I so interested in the art of conversation? It wasn't until my twenties that I realized that my social skills (or lack thereof) were starting to hold me back. I'd had my share of communication problems in high school and college, but once I was out in the real world, things got serious.

I knew I had talent to succeed at almost anything I set my mind to, but too often I would end up frustrating myself and others around me. Sometimes I even felt like a social outcast – I tried to make friends at work, for example, but never seemed to have more than a couple of buddies. It's no exaggeration to say that had I been better at holding conversations, listening to others, and resolving conflicts, my career would have taken off much earlier.

On the other hand, facing up to my problems kick-started an amazing journey of self-discovery. I'd always had an interest in psychology, but it took on a much greater significance once my future was on the line. If I was going to live up to my full potential, something had to change. Having learned so much – through reading books, watching videos, attending seminars, and making many mistakes along the way – I wanted to pass my hard-earned knowledge on to as many people as possible. Skeptical? It's time to think about a couple of erroneous beliefs that may be keeping you stuck in the same old comfort zone when it comes to communication. The first belief convinces you that communication isn't all that important in the first place. The second encourages a pessimism that can be fatal.

The Myth Of The Socially Awkward Genius

Some people know they are ineffective when it comes to making conversation and taking part in social situations, but console themselves with the thought that there is some kind of link between a high IQ and an inability to hold a decent conversation. TV shows such as *The Big Bang Theory* encourage us to believe that really smart people are often socially awkward, but that it doesn't really matter because they are extremely clever in other respects.

There are two problems with this line of thinking. The first is that there is no proven relationship between genius and poor social functioning. There are also numerous individual examples that go directly against this theory. Albert Einstein, commonly regarded as one of the most brilliant individuals to have ever lived, was charming and socially successful.[1] The second problem is that even if there were a proven negative correlation between IQ and degree of social skill, it's important to remember that most of us are not geniuses.

We couldn't all skate by on intelligence alone, even if it were enough to guarantee success in life. Given the fragile state of the human ego, this is a hard truth for some of us to swallow. Fortunately, whether or not you happen to be in possession of a brilliant mind, you can learn how to enjoy effective social interactions with others.

Can Conversation & Social Skills Be Taught?

If you've grown up with friends or relatives who have always excelled in social situations, you might think that social skills are innate – you've either got the talent required to talk with other people in a range of settings, or you haven't. This is a pretty depressing thought, but the

---

[1] Orzel, C. (2009). *The Myth of the Abrasive Genius*. scienceblogs.com

good news is that it isn't true! I know how it feels to compare yourself to others. My cousin Jason was always popular with his peers, his teachers adored him, and virtually all the adults in our family loved him too. If he hadn't been so nice, I would have really hated him. His mother always said that he'd just been blessed with natural charisma. Unfortunately, her choice of words made me believe that charm and social skill were fixed attributes.

Luckily, I came to realize that most people can improve if they are given the tools necessary to help themselves. There are so many communication experts out there – Julian Treasure, Evan Carmichael, and Tony Robbins are just three examples I can name off the top of my head – who have helped so many people. When I discovered the effect they have had on so many lives, I realized that I could also improve my social skills. Even if other people have told you that your conversation is flat and ineffective, you can choose to change. Today is the best time to start!

If you want further proof that social skills can be taught, consider the interventions offered to those with Asperger's Syndrome (AS). People with this diagnosis have a form of autism, a condition that impairs an individual's ability to communicate meaningfully with others. People with AS often talk excessively about their personal interests, have problems maintaining eye contact, speak in a monotonous tone of voice, and fail to take an interest in what others think and feel.[2] As a result, they often have problems forming bonds with others, which can cause loneliness and alienation from society.

The good news is that people with AS can be taught how to behave in social situations, which helps them form positive relationships. Through role play and training lead by trained therapists, they can learn how to "blend in" and function in most social settings.[3] What should we take from this? The moral of the story is clear - even if you are severely deficient in social skills, you can learn how to interact with others, as long as you have the necessary determination.

In conclusion, there's every reason to believe that you can learn to hold great

---

[2] NHS Choices. (2016). *Autism spectrum disorder (ASD)*. nhs.uk

[3] Miller, A., Vernon, T., Wu, A., & Russo, K. (2014). Social Skill Group Interventions for Adolescents with Autism Spectrum Disorders: A Systematic Review. *Review Journal Of Autism and Developmental Disorders, 1*, 254-265.

conversations, form solid relationships, and enjoy being around other people at both home and work. Even better – you'll get more accomplished with practice. Don't worry too much about the past. We've all had our fair share of embarrassing situations and social mishaps. That's totally normal! The most important thing is that you stop berating yourself for past mistakes, and get ready to change your approach to social interaction. Turn to the next chapter to discover how to build the perfect foundation for success.

Your Free Mindfulness E-book

I really appreciate the fact that you took an interest in my work!

I also think it's great you are into self-development and proactively making your life better.

Therefore, I would love to offer you a free, complimentary 120-page e-book.

It's about Mindfulness-Based Stress and Anxiety Management Techniques.

It will provide you with a solid foundation to kick-start your self-development success and help you become much more relaxed, while at the same time, becoming a more focused and effective person. All explained in plain English, it's a useful free supplement to this book.

To download your e-book, please visit:

http://www.tinyurl.com/mindfulnessgift

Enjoy!
Thanks again for being my reader! It means a lot to me!

Part I: Laying The Groundwork

Chapter 1: Listening – The Most Fundamental Of All Conversation Skills

Great conversation isn't just about what you say, but when you say it. We all know that a conversation is made up of two people speaking in turn, swapping information for mutual benefit and (hopefully) enjoyment. Unfortunately, too many of us don't actually listen to our conversation partner in the hope of understanding them. **In fact, we tend to listen just so we know when we can next take our own place in the spotlight without appearing too rude!** This means that two people can have what appears to be a conversation, but is in reality a simple game of "When do I next get to speak?" Obviously, this kind of "conversation" is a complete waste of time, because no one gets the chance to learn anything new, and no real relationship is forged.

Not only are many of us poor listeners, but we struggle to remember what other people are telling us. Speaker and communication expert Julian Treasure notes that although we spend approximately 60% of our total communication time listening to other people, we don't really pay attention. On average, we only retain 25% of what we hear.[4] He believes that we have gradually lost our capacity for high-quality listening over the years. Why? In brief, technology has made us lazy. Because we have become accustomed to using copies of information – books, videos, and so on – we subconsciously assume that it doesn't really matter whether we listen first time around, because we can always play or read it again later. The trouble is, of course, that you can't just Google a conversation you had later on and fill in the blanks. You need to be listening and paying attention in the present moment.

How To Practice Directing Your Attention

Luckily, you can retrain your brain to tune in and pay attention to any sound in your environment. Close your eyes, and take a moment to consider how many different "channels" or "streams" of sounds you can hear at any given moment. Give them labels – "people talking," "rain on the windows," and so on. This strengthens your ability to stay focused on what someone else is saying. Practice this exercise for several minutes each day, and you'll soon notice an

---

[4] Treasure, J. (2011). *5 ways to listen better*. https://youtu.be/cSohjlYQI2A

improvement in your ability to concentrate.

What Kind Of Listening Do You Need To Practice?

Did you know that there are several ways in which we can listen to one another? These approaches are called listening positions. When we listen, we can engage in critical versus empathetic listening, reductive versus expansive listening, and active versus passive listening. Most of us have heard about active and passive listening – and have been told that active listening is what we should always be doing – but listening is a little more complex than that.[5] In any given conversation, you might adopt a critical, reductive, and active position, for example.

When you listen from a critical position, you are analyzing the facts behind a situation. For example, if someone is telling you about the new phone they just bought and how its features make it better than all the other models on the market, you might be evaluating their points as they speak. You might consider whether the phone *really* has the largest screen size, the fastest processor, and so on. In this kind of situation, you are scanning each piece of information and forming your own conclusions.

In contrast, empathetic listening is the art of honoring feelings over bare facts. When you adopt an empathetic listening position, your main aim is to help someone express their feelings – simply by being present and paying attention. In focusing on someone's emotions, you will gain better insight into their thoughts and behaviors. This will show through in your facial expression, body language, and tone of voice. When your listening position is a good fit for the conversation topic and the other person's needs, you will both feel a sense of rapport.

You also need to understand the difference between reductive versus expansive listening. When you listen to someone in the hope that they'll get to the most important points as quickly as possible, you are engaging in reductive listening. This listening position is useful in high-pressure situations, and when you are dealing in objective facts. For example, a surgical nurse listening to the lead surgeon's instructions in the operating room needs to engage in reductive

[5] Nelson, V. (2017). *Conversations With Your College Student: What's Your Listening Position?* collegeparentcentral.com

listening. They must hone in on the facts as soon as possible, and then act upon them.

Reductive listening isn't appropriate if a speaker doesn't actually know what they think, what they want to say, or even how they feel. In this type of scenario, you need to take another approach. Instead of waiting for the other person to get right to the point, as you would when taking a reductive listening position, you need to sit patiently with the speaker as they work through their thoughts and feelings. This strategy is known as "expansive listening." Expansive listening is similar to empathetic listening in the sense that both positions accommodate the speaker's feelings, but the former is more focused on fact-finding than providing someone with an emotional outlet.

The final pair of positions – active versus passive listening – are the most well-known. In brief, active listening refers to the process of consciously making an effort to understand what the other person is saying and reacting in an encouraging manner, perhaps by summarizing and asking questions. By contrast, passive listening requires little effort. When you adopt a passive position, you may take some of the information in, but you aren't too bothered if you don't hear or fully understand it. Popular wisdom maintains that active listening is always preferable. This certainly isn't a bad rule to live by. After all, no one ever became offended because someone listened too well! But sometimes, passive listening is all that's needed. For example, if your father is telling you about his most recent day on the golf course – while knowing full well that you hate golf – you know that he's really talking for his own benefit, not yours. Taking a more passive approach would be fine in this case.

Learning about these positions gives you a quick troubleshooting tool to use the next time you feel as though a conversation isn't going smoothly, but you can't put your finger on why. Ask yourself, "Am I coming at this from the right listening position?"

Let's say that your friend is telling you about her divorce. She talks about how much money she will have to pay the lawyer, how many suspicious text messages she found on her soon-to-be ex-husband's phone, and so on – there is a lot of information coming from her mouth, and most of it is factual. You sit there, taking an active listening position. However, are you listening expansively or reductively, critically or empathically?

Your position will make all the difference in how your friend feels. If you are listening with the intention of just picking out the facts (e.g., how much the average divorce lawyer charges these days), or in the hope that she'll soon just get to the point (e.g. the date on which the divorce should actually be finalized), it will show in your demeanor. Your friend will see that you are listening, but she'll get the sense that you aren't really tuning in to her feelings – you are not taking the active, expansive, and empathetic position she needs. **If you get the feeling that someone feels as though you are not showing them enough care and understanding, check your listening position.** Are you more interested in how they are feeling, or are you just seeking out tidbits of gossip or intriguing facts?

Prepare To Be Surprised

Almost everyone has the power to shock. Always assume that when you begin a conversation with someone, you are there to learn something. If you start to view every conversation partner as a potential teacher, your social interactions will become much more enjoyable. You can even make a game of it. Ask yourself, "What might I learn from this person?" Once your conversation has come to a close, reflect on how they have challenged your worldview. Not every conversation is profound, but almost anyone can teach you something new.

Do You Even Need To Be In This Conversation?

If you are usually a good listener, but you find yourself shutting down when talking with someone else, consider the possibility that your brain is trying to tell you something. Our brains are smart – they have evolved to help us maximize our resources, including our concentration spans. If we noticed everything around us at all times, we'd become overloaded. This is why we have clever neurological circuits that allow us to disregard repetitive stimuli. For example, if we smell the same odor for more than a couple of minutes, we stop noticing it. That's why air fresheners are only noticeable for the first few minutes you are in a room. Similarly, if we hear the same sound over and over again, we stop registering it. It is as though your brain says, "OK! I've heard that so many times, I know what it's like, so I can switch off now."

This means that if a particular individual seems especially hard to listen to, it's possible that they have become somewhat repetitive. We are all guilty of telling the same stories on more than one occasion, and we all have our hot-button issues that trigger us to make the same old complaints (unless we practice sufficient self-awareness and avoid giving into the urges, of course). However, some people are especially inclined to tell you the same old thing over and over again. After a while, conversations with them are pretty pointless. I don't like to label people with words like "boring" or "dull," but some really are just that difficult to listen to. In other words, it's not you – it's them.

You have a couple of choices in such situations. Instead of beating yourself up for failing to listen properly, you can simply take a passive approach as they ramble on. This is only advisable if you absolutely must keep on good terms with the person involved, or value your relationship so highly that you are willing to be bored for a few minutes. For example, letting your spouse tell you the same story for the tenth time might just be the best option if it makes them happy.

The next option is to draw them onto another topic, which we will cover later in this book. The third option –the simplest and most effective of them all – is to bring the conversation to a close, or avoid getting hooked in the first place. Once you've heard the same old stories or opinions on countless occasions, you'll learn the words and phrases that will set them off. The moment you hear them, you can change the subject or make your excuses and leave. It will save you a lot of time! It's better to listen out for the warning signs than to resign yourself to yet another rendition of that anecdote you've heard on so many other occasions.

Never Try To Give The Appearance Of Paying Attention

In her TED talk, radio presenter Celeste Headlee spells out exactly what it takes to enjoy a great conversation. Naturally, she stresses the importance of listening. However, she also examines whether or not we should make the effort to look as though we are hanging on to someone else's every word. You may have been told to "look interested," to nod along when someone makes a point, and interject with phrases like "Oh really?" and "How fascinating!" at regular intervals. Headlee points out that instead of learning how to give the impression that you are paying attention, you should practice the art of *actually* paying attention.[6] Do not waste your precious mental energy worrying about the number of times you say "Oh really?" or whether you are nodding your head at the right moment. This will only distract you from your real mission, which is to work out what someone is trying to tell you. It's that simple, so don't try and make it more complicated. Incidentally, Headlee also believes that it's best to avoid someone altogether if you aren't prepared to listen to them. Otherwise, you're wasting everyone's time. Respect yourself and other people by actually making the effort to listen when someone has something important to say, but also knowing when to fold and walk away.

---

[6] Headlee, C. (2016). *10 ways to have a better conversation.* https://youtu.be/R1vskiVDwl4

Chapter 2: Tuning Up – How To Make Your Voice More Attractive

Along with your face, your voice is one of your most noticeable characteristics. You can be the most interesting person in the room, dressed smartly, and have great listening skills, but if your voice doesn't match up, people are unlikely to take you seriously. It might be unfair, but it's just human nature. Within seconds, we judge the quality of someone's voice. Luckily, you can use this to your advantage. In this chapter, you're going to learn why speaking in an attractive voice improves your chances of a good conversation and positive social interaction. Just think – by changing the way in which you speak, you could boost your social status instantly.

You should aim to develop your voice so that it is always audible, clear, and easy to understand. Even if you have an unusual accent, voice training can go a long way in helping you communicate with other people. The ideal voice reflects the speaker's personality. At the same time, it should always suggest that you are assertive and expressive. This doesn't mean that you have to shout and try to dominate the room. It means that you need to have confidence in both what you are saying and how you are saying it. Let's have a look at some of the most effective exercises that will change your voice for the better:

Loosen Your Lips

People with the most attractive voices enunciate their words clearly. When you listen to someone who pronounces their words perfectly, you are more likely to enjoy the conversation, even if you don't actually agree with what they are saying or find their personality off-putting. Along with good breathing, the key to good enunciation is to keep your tongue and lips relaxed. This trick also helps hide a lisp, which can increase your confidence if you suffer from this problem. If you tend to slur your words or just never sound them out properly, start practicing! Read passages from a book out loud when you are alone, or simply practice repeating common phrases. Notice how your mouth, throat, and chest feel when you enunciate your words. Over time, you will know what each word is supposed to feel like, and adjust your speech accordingly.

Breathe From Your Diaphragm

The most authoritative speakers breathe from their diaphragms, not their throats. If you want to speak in a rich, full voice that doesn't wobble or break, you need to breathe deeply and evenly. If your shoulders rise and fall with each breath, you are probably breathing from your upper chest rather than your abdomen.

To engage your diaphragm and help you learn to control your abdominal muscles, laugh silently. Close your mouth, and force yourself to laugh through your nose. Reading aloud can also help. Find a paragraph in a book or article that contains sentences of various lengths. Inhale from your diaphragm just before the start of each sentence, and exhale as you move towards the end. This will keep your voice nice and even.[7]

Hum & Sing

Most of us hum and sing when we're alone (or even with others!), so why not use it to practice varying the pitch of your voice? When you hum or sing your favorite songs, think about the variation in your voice. Do you have a good vocal range, or does it feel somewhat narrow and restricted? Experiment with the sounds you can make. There are few things so soul-destroying as being forced to listen to someone who speaks in a monotone. **You absolutely must learn how to vary your voice if you want other people to find you engaging.** Conversation is about melody as much as it is about content. Many of us have the habit of talking at a continually high pitch, which doesn't inspire confidence or communicate a sense of authority.

You shouldn't aim for a gravelly tone of voice – especially if you are woman – but in general, deep and rich is preferable to high and thin. Don't try to drastically change your pitch overnight. It will strain your voice, and your friends and family will probably ask you whether you've come down with a cold. Instead, work on lowering it slightly, then in a few days' time, lower it again. Practice singing an "ah" sound at various pitches. Do this exercise regularly, and you will gain total control over your pitch.

---

[7] Toastmasters International. (2017). *Your Speaking Voice.* toastmasters.org

Watch Your Intonation

Varying your pitch doesn't just make your speech easier and more pleasant to listen to. It also changes how people interpret your message. This can have serious consequences if you get it wrong. For example, take the following question:

"Will you be home by midnight?"

On the face of it, this looks like a neutral request for information. But what happens if you vary the intonation? If you asked the question in a flat, almost disinterested voice, the person you are asking might infer that you don't really care whether they make it home safely or not. They aren't exactly going to feel loved or cared for, and this might even lay the ground for an argument. Placing emphasis on specific words within the sentence gives a completely different impression. For example:

"*Will* you be home by midnight?"

"Will you be *home* by midnight?"

Say each version of this sentence aloud, and you will appreciate what a difference emphasis can make. In the first example, the speaker sounds a bit impatient or exasperated, as though they have already asked the other person for their schedule but have yet to receive the information. The second example implies that the speaker wants their conversation partner to come home, but they aren't convinced that it's going to happen – they want reassurance. **If you are talking to someone and they aren't reacting to you in the way you would expect, evaluate your intonation.** Are you inadvertently communicating a specific kind of meaning? Might your conversation partner be taking offense as a result?

Move Your Voice Forward

Do you produce sounds in your throat, or near the front of your mouth? Ideally, you should feel as though your words are formed on your lips, not in your throat. The secret is to relax your jaw and throat muscles. There's a simple but effective exercise you can use to do this. Lie on your back, and take deep breaths. Be sure to use your diaphragm. Always exhale through your mouth rather than your nose. Make a conscious effort to relax your jaw, mouth, and throat. Make sure that every exhalation feels smooth. Upon exhalation, say the "ah" sound. Repeat these steps a few times, keeping your mouth open. At no time should you feel as though your muscles are under any kind of strain. Next, count to five during each exhalation. Keep doing this until it feels natural and comfortable. You should be able to speak each number aloud without much effort. Remember, the point of this exercise is to train yourself how to relax your muscles so that your voice can flow freely. If it becomes difficult, you are probably not relaxed. You can also repeat this exercise sitting down and standing up.

Vocal training can work wonders, but don't overdo it. When you train your voice, you are forcing your vocal cords and muscles to work in new ways. It's important that you don't damage them. Toastmasters, the public speaking and leadership organization, tell their members to keep training sessions short (under five minutes) and to space them out over the day.[8]

Think About Rate & Timing

Take a moment to consider the way someone you really respect and admire sounds when they speak. Do they talk quickly, slowly, or somewhere in between? Most of us interpret a measured pace as a sign of confidence and authority. However, there isn't a single "best" speed that everyone should use. The world would be a very boring place if we all tried to conform to a prescribed speaking rate. If you are naturally outgoing, extroverted, or a quick thinker, you will probably speak faster than someone who is introverted or likes to consider all their options before opening their mouth. Most people utter between 120 and 190 words every minute, which is quite a wide variation.[9]

To find out whether you are a fast or slow speaker, find a passage in a book or article and read it aloud. Time yourself. Repeat this exercise a few times. Do the math to discover which category you fit into. You might be surprised by the results, because many of use aren't actually

---

[8] Ibid.
[9] Ibid.

familiar with how we sound. It's hard to change your natural speaking rate, but if you are breathing properly and enunciating your words, most people will still be able to understand what you are saying. If you are having an especially important conversation with someone, you can choose to speed up or slow down.

What if you don't happen to have an engaging voice, and the exercises above don't seem to help? No need to worry – you can hire a voice coach. Few of us are born with unusually attractive voices, but you can develop one with a little outside help. There's no need to feel embarrassed. Politicians and other people in the media spotlight get a little help all the time! They know that their public image depends in no small part on what they sound like, so if you suspect that your voice is holding you back, look up coaches and singing teachers in your area. If you enjoy the theater and performing, you could even take a few acting lessons.

Most singing teachers record their students during lessons, and then play the results back when assessing their pupil's progress. It becomes clear – sometimes painfully so – where you need to improve when you can actually hear your own voice. This isn't much fun at the beginning. Be prepared to exclaim, "Do I really sound like that?" I personally found vocal exercises a bit traumatic in the beginning. The first time I read through a speech then played it back to myself, I was horrified by just how squeaky my voice was. I liked to think that I spoke in deep tones. Needless to say, I was completely wrong. Luckily, I researched vocal exercises and have actually received compliments on my speaking voice! If I can do it, so can you.

If you recognize that you could use feedback from someone else but don't have the money or time to find and see a voice coach, ask the most eloquent friend or relative you have to give you some help. They might not know the mechanics of attractive speech, but they will still be able to correct you. Just be prepared for negative feedback. If you are going to ask someone to be honest, brace yourself for the possibility that you'll hear something that doesn't make you feel too good! Don't become discouraged. When you practice vocal exercises, you will soon start noticing a difference.

Sex Differences

As a general rule, both men and women receive more respect and attention when they speak in a warm, even tone of voice with suitable variation in pitch and tone. However, if you are looking to attract a member of the opposite sex, the picture changes slightly. For example, men tend to prefer women who speak at a higher pitch than men, and women seem to know this on an instinctive level – research shows that they automatically raise their voices when talking to a man they find attractive. Women are drawn to men who speak with a lower tone of voice. Scientists aren't quite sure why this is. It's possible that it comes down to desirable mate characteristics. Men tend to prefer women who appear youthful, and a breathy, high-pitched voice suggests a young, attractive appearance. Women tend to choose mates who are dominant, masculine, and self-assured, and a smooth, rich voice implies that a man possesses these traits.[10] However, both sexes can sound equally dominant. Whatever your sex, you can use your voice to project confidence.[11]

Size also comes into the equation. A deeper voice suggests a larger body size, whereas a higher pitch is associated with a smaller frame. Women usually look for men who are larger than the average woman, and vice versa for men.[12] This means that if you are a woman, making the effort to raise your pitch will make you more attractive and feminine-sounding. If you are a man, you should speak in a lower voice if you want a woman to find you appealing.

---

[10] Xu, Y., Lee, A., Liu, X., & Birkholz, P. (2013). Human Vocal Attractiveness as Signaled by Body Size Projection. *PLoS One*. https://doi.org/10.1371/journal.pone.0062397
[11] Hughes, S.M., Mogilski, J.K., & Harrison, M.A. (2014). The Perception and Parameters of Intentional Voice Manipulation. *Journal of Nonverbal Behavior, 38, 1,* 107-127.
[12] Ibid.

Chapter 3: Why You Should Take A Digital Detox – The Power Of Face-To-Face Interaction

Can you remember the days when people didn't use email, social media, and messaging apps as a substitute for conversation? If you're under the age of 25, life without Facebook is probably unimaginable. For those of us with a few more years on the clock, the rate of change in this domain has been staggering. I'm a big fan of technology, and love trying out new apps and sites that make my life easier. I wouldn't want to go back to the pre-Twitter era, and I think it's pretty cool that we can use the internet to talk to people around the world. However, there's a dark side to social media. Ironically, it's not doing our social skills any favors. If you want to be a great conversationalist, you need to keep technology in its proper place. It's time to step away from the screen and make time for regular face-to-face interaction.

How The Internet Is Killing Our Conversation Skills

Much has been written about why our online lives are damaging our social skills, but in my opinion it boils down to several key points: The internet impairs our ability to listen, it teaches us to be lazy thinkers, it destroys our ability to resolve conflicts in a constructive manner, and it sets us up to feel jealous of other people. This is a recipe for poor relationships and a lack of high-quality conversation. Did you know that we have a raging loneliness epidemic in the Western world? We've known for a long time that elderly people often suffer from loneliness, but now this problem is affecting millions of young adults too.[13] You might think that with all the technology we have available, no one would ever have to feel lonely again. But actually, the opposite is true. It seems harder to make and keep friends than ever before. So what has gone wrong?

Online, You Don't Have To Listen

As you know, two people need to listen to one another if they are going to have a decent conversation. Online, there's no obligation to even pretend that you're paying attention. We can skim over emails, read instant messages at our leisure, and flick back and forth between our

---

[13] Shoemaker, N. (2016). *Some Scientists Believe Loneliness is Becoming an Epidemic.* bigthink.com

friends' feeds and whatever we happen to be watching on YouTube. When we do want to pay attention to our friends, we can do so on our own terms. Needless to say, that's not how conversation should – or can – work in real life. But when you've become accustomed to switching your attention on and off when interacting with others, it becomes harder and harder to focus in face-to-face situations. Online, you are only a few clicks away from something more exciting. When this habit carries over into your regular life, you'll start wishing that your conversation partners would speak more quickly, or talk about a topic of special interest to you.

Online, You Don't Have To Think On Your Feet

Have you noticed that it's unusual to see people really trying to consider someone else's point of view in discussion forums? Occasionally two or more people might have a constructive back-and-forth about a particular topic, but more often, it descends into the written equivalent of folks speaking over one another. Usually, multiple people will randomly butt into the conversation. Think about it – is this a good substitute for real-life social interaction? Does it require sound conversation skills such as listening, thinking on your feet, and interpreting both verbal and nonverbal signals? I don't think so. If you tend to derive most of your social interaction from the internet, you are teaching yourself to be lazy. When confronted with the prospect of an actual conversation, you'll feel somewhat exposed and underprepared. Your conversations will lack the rapid exchange of ideas that make lively conversations so much fun.

When you're online, you are also let off the hook as far as critical thinking is concerned. If you don't want to put together a coherent argument that takes into account multiple perspectives, you can just say, "I'm out of here," which is the equivalent of shrugging your shoulders and saying, "Whatever." In real life, you probably wouldn't talk to other people like this. Online, you can take a break of minutes, hours, or even days before replying. You can use this time to gather your thoughts, put together a thoughtful response, and perhaps even use sound research to support your points. **That's great – everyone might learn something – but these skills hardly translate across to real life.** When you're in conversation with someone else face-to-face, you can't suddenly disappear for a few days. You have to face the music, be brave, and actually accept responsibility for your ideas.

Anything Goes On The Internet

Social media, and the internet in general, gives us an outlet for criticism, complaints, and even hate speech. Anyone who has been online for more than a couple of minutes knows that a sizeable proportion of the human race seem to think that it's fine to spew their hatred and venom on the internet. Even those of us who are generally nice, decent people are often guilty of dropping a sarcastic or unhelpful comment here and there. The problem is that when you type from the anonymity of a computer, you aren't held to account for your behavior. In fact, plenty of people don't even bother hiding behind the cloak of pseudonyms these days. They just type hateful tweets under their own names, or post aggressive messages on Facebook. I can't find any research on adult-on-adult cyberbullying, but surveys show that approximately 10% of young adults have both bullied, and been bullied, online.[14] Judging from anecdotes I've heard from my friends and clients, I don't think this problem goes away in adulthood!

Sure, if you say something particularly awful on the internet, you might face repercussions. However, for the most part, you can get away with being overly critical, abrupt, and rude in many internet spaces. Online, you don't have to face social disapproval. You don't have to justify your opinions. You can just dump them and run away – there is no obligation to return to a thread or comments section.

This isn't to say that you should always be nice to everyone, all the time. If you wouldn't mind saying it in person, then it's probably reasonable to say it online. But so many of us forget to follow this simple rule, and it results in hurt feelings and pointless arguments. Worse, we forget how to actually argue and solve problems via proper conversations. This sets us up for a fall when we come up against interpersonal issues in the real world.

Why Social Media Makes You Feel Inferior To Others

Another problem you'll come up against if you spend too much time online? Social comparisons and feelings of envy. In case you didn't already know, social media tends to reflect

---

[14] Hemphill, S.A., & Heerde, J.A. (2014). Adolescent Predictors of Young Adult Cyberbullying Perpetration and Victimization Among Australian Youth. *Journal of Adolescent Health, 55, 4,* 580-587.

the highlights of someone's life, not their bad days. Yes, there are people who use it to express how unhappy they are and voice their every grievance, but the majority use it as a promotional platform. They post photos of positive life events such as a new job, moving to a new home, getting engaged, and so on. It's so easy to look at their upbeat posts and take them at face value. Even if we like to think that we're a good judge of character, we tend to fall into the comparison trap.

Appearances can be deceptive. Yes, your friend may have won that hard-earned promotion, but they may also be on the edge of a nervous breakdown from working the long hours that come with it. Now, here's the kicker – if you don't actually have conversations with people face-to-face, you are unlikely to know the full story. **Conversation diminishes jealousy, because it allows you to gain a more authentic insight into someone else's life.** When you take time to get to know someone, you realize that they have their share of struggles. It also allows you to build richer relationships. Rather than wait for social media updates, why not have proper conversations on a regular basis? You'll be able to practice your social skills, and you'll also feel less inclined to compare yourself to others.

In case you need convincing further, here's a shocking finding published in the journal *Psychology of Popular Media Culture:* When college students view social media profiles of (fictitious) people who apparently enjoy great health and social popularity, their self-esteem plummets.[15] If a single profile can trigger these effects, imagine what Facebook will do to your mental health if you spend too much time browsing other peoples' profiles. It's time to take a step back.

The Simple Solution: A Digital Detox

So what should we do? Quite simply, we need to think twice before spending hours "talking" to other people online. Last year, I tried a digital detox for the first time. Obviously, I couldn't quit the internet entirely – I need it for work, and I couldn't ignore my best friend's WhatsApp messages. However, I stopped logging into Facebook, I ignored Instagram, I cut my

[15] Vogel, E.A., Rose, J.P., Roberts, L.R., & Eckles, K. (2014). Social Comparison, Social Media, and Self-Esteem. *Psychology of Popular Media Culture, 3, 4,* 206-222.

Twitter usage down to ten minutes per day, and I didn't initiate text-based conversations with anyone. I vowed to detox for a week, and see how it made me feel.

I'll be honest – at first, I felt very isolated. I missed seeing what my friends were up to on Facebook, and the feeling that I might be missing out on something gnawed away at me. But then I had a revelation. If I really cared about what was happening in my friends' lives, I could arrange to see them in person! To my alarm, I realized that although I live pretty close to most of them, it had been a while since we'd spent quality time together. I was feeling lonely by Day 3, so I put in a call to a buddy I hadn't seen in a few weeks. She was surprised to hear from me, but also delighted that I'd bothered to call her and ask to meet for a drink instead of firing off a few short messages.

We met at a local coffee shop and talked for a couple of hours about work, dating, and even current affairs. I left feeling positively uplifted. I'd forgotten how good it felt to have a proper conversation. Yes, it's much harder to arrange to see someone and actually speak to them than it is to send a text message, audio clip, or a Facebook "like." But is it more rewarding? Definitely. The fact is, we speak much faster than we type, and so much of the meaning shared during conversation is in intonation and body language. It just isn't the same as actually sitting opposite one another.

Taking digital detoxes helps keep my conversation skills sharp, because it forces me to actually get out there and interact with people in real time. I can't hide behind a screen – when you have a proper conversation, you have to think about what you are saying, as you are saying it. This means that you have to make the effort to communicate your ideas clearly, speak in proper sentences, and put together coherent arguments on the spot.

The more uncomfortable the thought of a detox makes you feel, the more urgently you need to take a social media holiday. If your friends and family live far away, and social media is your only means of communication, you can go on a modified detox instead. Use Skype or another similar app and use video rather than text.

Cut Down On The Unnecessary Emails

Finally, I want to make a point about online communication in the workplace. Perhaps this situation sounds familiar. You are working in the office, or maybe even at home. You get a notification of a new email or instant message. It's from a co-worker or family member – who just so happens to be a few meters away! It sounds ludicrous, but many of us are so reluctant to actually get up and talk to people that we'd rather type a message instead, even when it would be quicker to rise from our chairs and deliver it in person.

From this point forward, vow that whenever you have the opportunity, get up from your chair and *talk to someone*. Our great-grandparents would be shocked if they saw how humans in the developed world "speak" to one another these days. No wonder there are so many lonely people out there, despite the fact that our world population is growing daily, and more people have access to the internet than ever before. You don't have to forsake social media altogether, but if you want to develop your conversation skills, consider logging on a little less often.

Chapter 4: How To Stop Fearing Judgment

Most people struggle not only with difficulty in finding the right words in conversation, but they are also terrified of being judged. In some cases, this can be completely paralyzing. People with Social Anxiety Disorder (SAD) suffer from this to an extreme degree. They often have panic attacks in social situations, or even suffer panic attacks that are triggered by the mere thought of having to talk to others. What they actually fear is not the act of conversation. They are more worried about being judged, or seen as "wrong" in some way.

The implications are obvious. SAD can lead to complete social isolation, because sufferers would rather avoid social interaction altogether than risk being on the receiving end of negative judgments.[16] In all probability, you don't have SAD (although if a fear of social situations is holding you back and causing you to have panic attacks, you should see a doctor), but you might still be worried what other people will think of you. It's natural to care whether people like you. No one likes to be a social outcast. The problem comes when you care so much about other people's judgments that you stop expressing your opinions, and lose out on the chance to start or build relationships.

I'm not going to lie – people do judge, and they will form their own opinions about you. These opinions are shaped by your looks, your mannerisms, what you say, how you behave, and dozens of other characteristics. It would be silly (and dishonest) of me to pretend that you can win the hearts and minds of everyone you meet. Just as you have the right to decide whether or not you want to be someone's friend, they also have the right to make up their own mind about you. As the saying goes, you can't please all of the people all of the time. But you can choose to accept yourself, grow your self-confidence, and learn how to let go of even the harshest of judgments.

Step One – Build Self-Confidence

When you really and truly accept yourself, you will be less troubled by what other people

---

[16] Stein, M.B., & Stein, D.J. (2008). Social anxiety disorder. *The Lancet, 371*, 1115-25.

think. If you are content and secure in your own skin, the prospect of being judged won't really bother you. Sure, you might still be offended if someone says something unkind, but it won't rattle you for long. You'll be able to pick yourself up, dust yourself down, and remember that although you aren't perfect, you are just fine as you are.

Don't worry, I'm not just going to tell you to accept yourself and then skip ahead to the next step. I'm going to give you some useful starting points.

1. *Challenge your self-talk*. If someone were to stand next to you all day, muttering or even shouting insults in your ear several times per hour, you probably wouldn't feel too great about yourself by the time evening rolled around.

   Yet lots of us do this to ourselves! If you tend to berate yourself, put yourself down, or dwell on your failures and mistakes, you don't stand a chance of developing true confidence. I'm not saying that you have to compliment yourself all day, but you need to realize that negative self-talk will kill your self-esteem and your chances of social success. Distract yourself, replace the insults with neutral statements, say "STOP!" out loud, see a therapist, or do whatever you have to do to fix this issue. Eliminating negative self-talk also helps you realize when someone is bullying or insulting you.

   Some people are so used to putting themselves down that they can't actually tell when someone else is behaving badly – after all, no one can say anything worse than what is already going through their heads. This leaves them vulnerable to abusive and toxic relationships.

2. *Get good at something*. You know that warm feeling you get when you've succeeded in picking up a new skill? That feeling is a great basis for self-confidence. Learn something new, because it will shore up your self-belief.

   You'll feel proud of yourself because you will have proven, without a doubt, that you are a capable person who can develop themselves and their talents. Not only that, but your new interest will give you some high-quality conversation material. Get a regular hobby, and you'll never again be stuck for something to say in response to the question, "So, what have you been up to recently?"

3. *If you can change something – change it!* In theory, you could be judged on almost anything – your hair, your opinions, your job – you name it, someone can judge you on it.

In most cases, there's very little you can (or should) do about it. For example, if someone finds you ugly, that's their opinion – there's nothing (aside from cosmetic surgery or heavy makeup, maybe) that you can do to change their minds. Even if you could, why waste time catering to someone else's aesthetic preferences? However, there are some traits and characteristics that you can change, not only to avoid judgment, but to develop yourself as a person. For instance, if you have a specific fear that other people will think you are boring or ignorant, you can make the decision to become more interesting and more informed about the world.

This would be a win-win solution. Whether or not someone else decided you were boring or ignorant, you would feel good about yourself, knowing that you were becoming more entertaining and educated by the day.

Should You Fake It 'Til You Make It?

Some books will tell you that if you feel uneasy or panicky in social situations, the answer is just to pretend that you feel confident. However, if you've ever suspected that most people (especially highly sensitive and empathetic individuals) are good at detecting false confidence and bravado, you're right. If you think that you can get away with trying to fake your way to good self-esteem, you're wrong. Lots of people will see straight through you. Even if you happen to have outstanding acting skills, pretending to be someone else is just plain tiring.

After a while, the mask will slip, which will reveal how hard you've been trying all along. Using a fake persona will also leave you feeling like a fraud. You'll start to worry that people will judge you for being inauthentic, which will just add to your problems. Good communication, just like a good relationship, is rooted in authenticity. When we try and quash our true selves, we get uncomfortable. The fear of being "found out" is never far away. In conclusion, I decided long ago that the cliché, "Fake it 'til you make it," isn't very good advice.

Here's some research to back up this point. A recent paper published in the *Journal Of Personality* shows that people judge the self-esteem of someone they have just met within a minute of exposure.[17] What's more, their judgments are usually accurate. That's right – when you meet someone new, they can tell within 60 seconds whether you hold yourself in high or low regard.

You have probably experienced this for yourself. For example, I recently met my mother's new neighbor for the first time whilst taking a trip back home. I was struck by how confident and secure he appeared. I immediately found myself thinking, "This guy was probably someone pretty special back in the day." I found myself drawn to him, and we must have chatted for at least quarter of an hour. Over coffee, my mother told me that her new neighbor was a retired Sheriff. It made complete sense, given his demeanor.

So why is it that some people appear more confident? The authors of the study believe that people subconsciously gather and analyze a lot of information within that first minute. When I met my mother's neighbor, I picked up on several clues that told me a lot about his self-image. He spoke with an even, deep voice. His posture was excellent for his age and condition, and he spoke without hesitation or any filler words. I have no idea whether this guy had ever taken a public speaking class or a self-development course. You know what? It doesn't matter.

Whether he is naturally confident or cultivated it over time, the result is the same – he seems completely at ease with himself and others. With respect to the Sheriff, I doubt he was also an Oscar-winning actor – his self-belief was real.

---

[17] Hirschmüller, S., Schmukle, S. C., Krause, S., Back, M. D., & Egloff, B. (2017). Accuracy of Self-Esteem Judgments at Zero Acquaintance. *Journal of Personality*.

Step Two – Stop Making Everything About You

You should know by now that I'm not one to beat about the bush. I'm going to be blunt here – if you are always worrying about whether other people are judging you, you're self-obsessed. When you ruminate about what everyone else thinks about you, you're basically saying, "Other people sure do think a lot about me. They probably put a lot of effort into formulating an opinion. What others think is really important. I really matter to them."

I hate to break it to you, but you aren't actually the center of the universe. Yes, we are all social beings who tend to judge others. However, once you have left the room or ended the conversation, the other person probably isn't going to spend hours thinking about you and your faults. Even if you were to say something incredibly stupid at a party and the host then laughed about it with their friends the next day, they probably wouldn't give it much thought after that. People move on. Like you, they have their own lives to lead.

When you find yourself sinking into a self-analytic rut, try this simple trick - focus on other people instead. **If you're talking to someone and feel as though they might be judging you, challenge yourself to learn more about them.** See what you can discover about their lives, their opinions, and their favorite activities. This halts your self-obsession. Furthermore, you'll probably discover that they are - gasp! – a complex, flawed human being like yourself. It's always comforting when we realize that someone who seems intimidating or judgmental is really just another person, with their unique set of strengths and weaknesses. The more we get to know someone, the friendlier they usually seem.

Here's a final thought. Remind yourself that most of the judgments other people make are never shared. For example, you'll probably never know what a person at the party thought of you. The clerk at the store, the acquaintance you bumped into at a conference, even your closest friends – they are unlikely to tell you exactly what they think. There is precisely nothing you can do about this. You aren't the thought police, so why worry? As the old saying goes, what you don't know can't hurt you. As long as someone isn't being a jerk, give them permission to have their own opinions! You can't force them to change their minds, so just let it be.

What About Rejection?

When someone turns you down for a date, a job interview, a joint vacation, or anything else that means something to you, it's natural to be hurt. When someone rejects you, it's easy to assume that they have weighed up the pros and cons of each option and decided that you just aren't good enough. No doubt about it, rejection stings. I'm not about to argue otherwise. Did you know that the same parts of the brain responsible for sensations of physical pain are also activated when we experience social rejection?[18] If you've had a pain in your chest that made it seem as though your heart was in danger of breaking, you'll know this for yourself.

However, you have a choice to make when you are rejected. You may not have had a say in the other person's decision, but it's up to you to frame the situation in a way that helps you take a more balanced perspective. Let's say that you are at a party, talking with someone you find really attractive. Everything is going well. By the end of the evening, you've been chatting for several hours and have both had a few drinks. Although you feel nervous, you decide to ask them for a date the following Saturday. Unfortunately, they turn you down. They tell you that although they are flattered, they don't think it would be a good idea. Shortly afterwards they leave, never to be seen again. In case you're wondering – yes, this has happened to me. I was 22 at the time, and it hurt like heck. When it happened, I automatically assumed that she didn't find me attractive, and I even started wondering whether I was ugly. I couldn't wait to get home that night and bury myself under the covers! For the next few weeks, I felt very self-conscious about my looks. But let's look at the variety of ways in which I could have framed this situation:

1. "She rejected me because although we had a great time, she thinks I am ugly."

2. "She rejected me because she doesn't want to date or have a boyfriend at this point."

3. "She rejected me because although she likes me, she sensed we might not be romantically compatible."

---

[18] Pond, R., Richman, S., Chester, D., & DeWall, N. (2014). Social Pain and the Brain: How Insights from Neuroimaging Advance the Study of Social Rejection. In Duric, D. (Ed.), *Advanced Brain Neuroimaging Topics in Health and Disease – Methods and Applications*. DOI: 10.5772/58271

4. "She rejected me because she has a boyfriend, and she just wanted an ego boost whilst at the party."

I'm sure you can think of many other possibilities to add to the list.

It doesn't matter whether or not you ever discover the truth. What matters is that you realize that you can control your response, and that's an empowering place to be. Not all rejection stems from a place of negative judgment. What's more, even if it does, that doesn't mean it's going to happen again in the future. OK, the girl may have found me ugly. But does that logically mean that every woman on earth shares the same opinion? Given that I've dated quite a few women, the answer would have to be, "No."

By the way, a few years later I found out that the girl at the party was "on a break" from her boyfriend. They had a pretty rocky relationship, but they got married in the end! Who was I to stand in the path of true love? That episode taught me a valuable lesson about rejection. Sometimes, you have no idea what's really going on behind the scenes.

Chapter 5: Using Empathy In Conversation

What's the most powerful force that can connect two people? Love, friendship, a shared goal? Maybe. Personally, I believe that empathy is the glue that really holds relationships together. Empathy is the ability to enter into someone else's frame of reference. When you show empathy, you don't just listen to whatever it is they have to say. You don't try to understand it from a purely intellectual point of view. To be empathetic is to actively try and adopt the other person's position.[19]

If you are just chatting about casual matters, you don't need to worry too much about being empathetic. It's when you start talking about the bigger stuff that empathy really makes the difference between an "OK" conversation and a meaningful connection. If you've ever come away from a deep exchange feeling truly heard and understand, it's probably because your conversation partner showed you empathy. Empathy creates a safe environment. It allows other people to open up, even when talking about their deepest emotions or most unpleasant memories. This sets the stage for life-changing relationships. If you want to help someone out, you will need to understand what the problem is in the first place. The best way to get inside their head is through harnessing your natural empathy. It's powerful stuff!

Showing Empathy In Conversation

How can you signal that you are ready and willing to take an empathetic stance? If you sense that someone wants to open up to you, here's how you can take steps towards understanding someone else's position.

1. Don't speak badly of others. Keep your tone nonjudgmental. Other peoples' actions and behaviors tend to come up in all kinds of conversation. Everyone gossips from time to time. However, if you want someone to feel comfortable in opening up to you, you need to fight the urge to talk badly of others. Who is going to feel safe talking to you if you repeatedly demonstrate a willingness to stab other people in the back? No one feels safe opening up to

---

[19] Benbassat, J., & Baumal, R. (2004). What Is Empathy, and How Can It Be Promoted during Clinical Clerkships? *Academic Medicine, 79, 9,* 832-839.

someone judgmental, because they worry that they'll also be judged! Obviously, you should also abstain from passing judgment on what your conversation partner is telling you. You should also refrain from giving unsolicited advice. Assume that if they want you to make a suggestion, they'll ask for it.

2. Show that you are taking an expansive listening position. Remember, an expansive listening position is one in which you happily and patiently follow the listener's train of thought, without judgment. If you show even the merest hint of impatience, the other person will shut down. They will assume that you would rather get the conversation over and done with. This isn't going to encourage them to trust you.

3. Ask them directly but gently whether there's something on their mind. If your conversation partner seems a little distracted, and their body language is tense, ask them whether there's anything they would like to talk about. Don't be aggressive about it. Just give them the chance to speak if they would like to do so. Of course, if they tell you that something is bothering them but they would rather not discuss it, you should show empathy by telling them that you understand, and if they change their mind they can still come and talk to you.

4. Give them time to "empty the tank." When was the last time someone truly listened to you, without leaping in with an interruption or judgment? We all know that sometimes, we just want to tell someone exactly what we are thinking and feeling. If we are lucky, they will have empathy for our position, and go out of their way to give us as much space as we need. If you find yourself occupying the role of listener, allow the other person to say all the things they need to say. When you interrupt someone, you are signaling to them that your personal thoughts are more important than their right to speak. This isn't the message you want to send.

5. Try to show Unconditional Positive Regard (UPR). The humanistic therapist Carl Rogers used a concept called Unconditional Positive Regard when talking with his clients. He believed that everyone has all the resources they need to sort out their own problems, but sometimes they need the right kind of environment in which to work out the best solution.[20] This is a really

[20] Rogers, C.R. (2007). The Necessary and Sufficient Conditions Of Therapeutic Personality Change. *Psychotherapy: Theory, Research, Practice, Training, 44, 3,* 240-248.

helpful framework if you are trying to take an empathetic stance. Just as Rogers did, make a decision to accept the other person just as they are, regardless of their speech or actions. This doesn't mean that you have to agree with what they have done, and it doesn't mean you should let them act in a threatening or inappropriate way. Think of UPR as a tool you can use to leave your personal biases to one side, and approach the conversation from a receptive point of view. When you work from the assumption that the other person is at heart a good, rational individual with the capacity for change, you likely to show them true acceptance and react in an empathetic manner.

What To Say When You're Told Something Shocking

Empathy is one of the greatest gifts one person can give another, but it should come with a warning label. When you create a safe space for someone, there's every chance that they will share their deepest personal secrets with you. This won't always make for easy listening. Some of these secrets will be sad, but relatively "normal." Experiences that most of us can relate to, such as feeling hopeless after losing a job, or feeling deeply depressed after breaking up a with partner, fall into this category.

On other occasions, you might find that your conversation partner tells you something that shocks you. No matter how prepared you think you are, or how much life experience you have accumulated, sometimes it only takes a few seconds for a conversation to take a surprising turn. You might not be able to contain your outrage or sadness. As long as you don't make your own emotions the center of the conversation, it's fine to let the other person know how you feel. You are not a robot. A simple statement such as, "To me, that sounds terrible," or "I can't help feeling sad for you" will leave them in no doubt that you care, but at the same time draws a firm line between their feelings and your own.

Always aim for honesty. If they ask you how their revelation makes you feel, let them know. Be authentic and open with your emotions, because this in turn will allow the other person to feel safe in telling you what is going on in their mind and heart. If you can't help but react strongly to something you are told, make sure that you tell the other person that they aren't to blame. Tell them that you are honored that they chose to open up to you, and emphasize that your feelings are yours alone to deal with.

Sometimes, the best answer is actually no answer at all. Remember, people do not always open up because they want or need someone to tell them what to do. Often, they open up because they feel the need to be heard. A simple gesture can also do well in place of words. A light touch on their arm, a slow nod of the head, or even a hug (if you already have a close relationship with the person) can provide a lot of comfort.

Know When To Bite Your Tongue

What if you understand precisely what another person is experiencing, or share a similar history? For example, when someone reveals that they lost their mother as a teenager, you might be quick to reassure them that you know what they went through if you lost your father at the age of twenty. I really do understand the urge to make a connection and to find common ground. But you need to proceed with care. Even if your experience sounds similar to theirs, even if you feel as though you can empathize on many levels, you are two distinct individuals. You have different personalities, backgrounds, ambitions, and priorities. If you are too quick to draw a parallel between their experiences and your own, you run the risk of appearing insensitive.

Consider the situation from another angle. Have you ever poured your heart out to someone, or explained how a traumatic event made you feel, only to hear, "I know exactly what you are going through! I had the same thing happen to me. Back in the day, I..." and so on. You might have ended up just sitting there whilst they told you their own story. Even worse, you might have ended up comforting them!

Do you ever dive in with a quick, "Me too!" and end up launching into a story of your own? Don't worry if the answer is a resounding, "Yes." No one is perfect. I know I've done this on occasion. When my friend Sam lost out on an apartment he really wanted to rent, he was bemoaning his bad luck over a coffee. The poor guy only got a couple of minutes of airtime before I explained that back in college, I'd missed out on my first choice of accommodation. Therefore, I told him, I could relate to his experience. Sam was too polite to tell me to shut up, but I later realized how insensitive I had been. Luckily for me, he's very forgiving. On a couple of occasions, I've even come close to making the same mistake with my clients. When someone tells me that they have suffered from low self-esteem since they were a teenager, I'm always tempted to say, "Me, too!" and tell them all about my adolescent experiences. I'll never lose the urge completely, but I've got it under control. I remind myself that the conversation isn't about me. If a session triggers some difficult memories, I debrief later with a friend, or just take some time out to relax and process anything that came up. Of course, if someone asks you, "Do you know what I mean?" or "I don't know if you've ever experienced anything like this?" then feel free to share your own story.

Don't be surprised if you feel drained after a deep conversation. Sometimes, showing empathy may be as simple as commiserating with a co-worker over heavy traffic on the route to work. It doesn't take much effort to empathize with this kind of situation, and it is unlikely to sit with you once the conversation has ended. On the other hand, listening to someone talk about a bereavement, serious illness, or a divorce requires some serious emotional labor.

You don't have to be a human sponge. If you know that you are likely to have a deep discussion with someone when you next meet up, schedule some time alone for a couple of hours afterwards. From time to time, I work with clients who have histories of complex psychological and emotional problems. These often stem from traumatic incidents. The stories they tell me are literally hair-raising. I'm happy to be empathetic and help them work through their problems, but I've realized that for the sake of my own emotional health, I need some time alone after our sessions. Those of us who work with people facing tough times in their lives need to decompress regularly, or compassion fatigue can set in.[21] Never forget that your own well-being is just as important as that of anyone else.

---

[21] Benson, J., & Magraith, K. (2005). Compassion fatigue and burnout. *Australian Family Physician, 34, 6.*

Chapter 6: How To Let Go – Why You Don't Need To Share All Your Ideas

Sometimes, it feels almost impossible to keep a conversation going. (Don't worry if you have this difficulty – later in the book, I'll show you how to keep any conversation alive.) On the other hand, there are those of us who actually have the opposite problem. The conversation seems to be moving too fast, and we want to jump right in whilst someone else is still speaking.

Of course, you already know that interrupting someone is the height of rudeness. Yet it's easy to fall into the trap of voicing every thought that pops into your head. We all do it – there are no sex differences when it comes to interruption frequency, and studies show that everyone from young children to adults do it.[22] This bad habit can turn even the best conversations sour. When you feel as though you are in rapport with another person, it can seem as though the pair of you share many of the same ideas and experiences. So what do you do? Rush to share your own stories, of course!

Unless you are accomplished in keeping a clear head and maintaining control over your feelings (for example, if you are well versed in the art of mindfulness), your mind will take you down all kinds of tangents. This is totally normal. In itself, it's no problem. The trouble starts when you feel the need to tell everyone what's going through your head. You may intend to add a quick anecdote or point to the conversation but, before you know it, you've completely hijacked the discussion.

What Goes Through Your Head When Someone Else Is Speaking?

To fully appreciate how hard it is to refrain from diving into a conversation, let's consider what tends to run through our heads when we listen to someone else speak.

1. The desire to express total agreement. A lot of us are quick to make it clear when we agree with something. We like someone to know that we are on their team, that we know what exactly what they mean, and that we approve of their opinions. This makes sense, given that most of us

---

[22] Marche, T.A., & Peterson, C. (1993). The Development and Sex-Related Use of Interruption Behavior. *Human Communication Research, 19, 3,* 388-408.

thrive on approval and compliments. If we like positive feedback, then other people must like it too – right? Yes, but only in an appropriate context. There is no value in barging in to a conversation just to explain why you think the speaker is completely correct in everything that they say.

2. *The desire to express total disagreement.* If someone is making a point that goes against our own belief system, the temptation to tell them precisely why they are so wrong can feel overwhelming. We seem to believe that if we can just make them see things from our point of view – say, within the next three minutes – they will immediately retract their statement and agree that our own opinion is far superior to theirs. If you think about it, this never works in practice, but it doesn't stop us from wanting to try.

3. *The desire to correct the speaker on a trivial point.* If you have a pedantic streak, you will pick up on small inconsistencies or errors, such as a mispronunciation or a minor error regarding a date or name. There is never a good reason to leap in with a minor correction. All you will gain is a reputation as an annoying pedant who can't see the wood for the trees. Pedantry is so irksome because it diminishes the point someone is trying to make, which disrupts the flow of conversation and undermines rapport.[23] If you act in a pedantic manner, people will begin to suspect that you just enjoy making others angry. It doesn't matter if you just want to help – keep quiet.

4. *The desire to sling a well-timed insult or cutting remark.* For those of us who enjoy banter and wordplay, an opportunity for a witty remark or retort is almost irresistible. If you are the type of person who loves to make others laugh, you need to remember that the speaker's right to have their say is more important than your right to flaunt your excellent sense of humor. It's a matter of respect. If your sense of humor is really that great, then you can rest assured that it's only a matter of time before you come up with another hilarious remark that you can share with others.

5. *The desire to ask a question about a topic, even though the speaker has moved on.* If you are

_____

23 Jabour, B. (2014). *So you're a pedant? It's nothing to be proud of.* theguardian.com

actively listening to a speaker in the hope of expanding your knowledge of a particular subject, you might have a few questions you'd like to ask. However, by the time you have formulated a great question, they will probably have started talking about something else! The best solution is to note it down. Forcing a speaker to return to ground they have already covered will break their mental flow. If you've been on the receiving end, you'll know just how annoying this is.

6. *The desire to make "helpful" practical suggestions as to how the speaker could solve a problem.* If you are the sort of person who enjoys solving problems and likes to help other people, you might want to share a possible solution to an issue raised by the speaker. You might have the best intentions in the world, but unless someone asks for your advice, they probably don't want it. You might also be interested to know that when the average person gets some unsolicited advice that goes against their own impression of a situation, they are quite likely to reject it out of spite! So, unless someone has asked you for your input, it's often pointless to impose your own opinions anyway.[24]

If you really must pass on your idea, wait until they have finished speaking, ask whether they would like to hear your opinion, and then present your thoughts in a succinct manner if appropriate. Don't worry about letting some of your ideas go. You are bound to have lots more in the future.

7. *The desire to answer a rhetorical question.* Rhetorical questions are intended to encourage the listener to think about a topic from a new perspective. They are not intended to be used as conversation starters. If you want to answer a rhetorical question, you can do so – in your head.

How To Keep Quiet

I used to be a chronic interrupter. If someone ever told me a story, I would often add my own contributions as they were speaking. Until my twenties, I believed that this tendency was just a sign of my enthusiasm. It wasn't until a friend pulled me aside after a dinner party one night to ask whether I realized how much air I was sucking out of the room that the penny

---

[24] Fitzsimons, G.J., & Lehrman, D.R. (2004). Reactance to Recommendations: When Unsolicited Advice Yields Contrary Responses. *Marketing Science, 23, 1,* 82-94.

dropped. I trusted the friend in question, so my embarrassment was enough to get me to quit virtually overnight. Sometimes it takes a bit of tough love before we fully appreciate where we've been going wrong. Asking a close friend for their honest opinion is a good step. Brace yourself for their feedback! If they confirm that yes, you are indeed an interrupter, ask for their help. Agree on a simple hand signal they can use whenever you start hijacking a conversation. You will soon start to see (quite literally) how and when you tend to interject, and this awareness will help you make changes.

Changing my attitude to thinking and conversation also made it easier to let go of my thoughts. Everyone has hundreds of thousands of thoughts every single day, and most are unremarkable. They come and go. The next time you have a few minutes to yourself, just watch your own mind. A whole range of words, images, and ideas will flash in and out of your conscious awareness. Most aren't really that interesting, and hardly any stick around longer than a couple of seconds.

This exercise helped me work out that just because I might have a thought, there is no reason to assume that it must be shared with the world. Everyone has their own stream of consciousness. Thoughts are transient. I realized that if I was still hung up on an issue by the time the speaker had finished taking their turn in conversation, it was probably important enough for me to bring up. The next time you feel tempted to interrupt someone, sit with the thought instead. You'll be surprised at how much junk flies through your head, and how you'll soon realize that you wouldn't have added anything to the conversation by sharing it with everyone else.

Discretion Is The Better Part Of Valor

Not only do you have to know when to keep your ideas to yourself, but you should also know when to avoid gossiping about other people, or passing on confidential information. I get it – it's human nature to gossip. Reality TV shows are incredibly popular, and for good reason. We all want to know who hates who, who loves who, and so on. When we learn a secret about a friend or relative, the temptation to pass it on can feel almost overwhelming. For some reason, negative gossip is even more alluring than good news.

Knowing when to stay quiet is partly a matter of maturity. As you get older, you start to realize that sometimes, it really is best to keep schtum. The short-term joy of passing on a secret isn't usually worth the eventual fallout. You can be assured that when you divulge someone's secret, it will come back to bite you. Maybe not within a week, month, or even a year, but gossips seldom get away with their bad habit for long. Even if you manage to avoid offending a specific person, you will slowly gain a reputation as an untrustworthy individual.

If you're talking to someone and are on the verge of giving away a confidential or highly personal piece of information concerning another individual, ask yourself these questions:

1. Why am I so keen to share this piece of information right now? Unless the other person absolutely needs to know a secret, there is no reason why you should pass it on. Ask yourself what your motives really are. This might not be the easiest question to answer, because your reflections might reveal some rather unflattering truths. For example, you may be forced to admit that your primary motive is to get some kind of revenge on the person you are about to betray. However, passing on confidential information isn't going to help. You need to actually get to the bottom of the dispute, and resolve it at the source. Don't drag an innocent third party into the situation. Or perhaps you are feeling low in confidence and want to make yourself look better in comparison to someone else, so you decide to spill the beans about their disastrous personal life. Again, what's the underlying issue here? In this case, you would need to address your low self-esteem, pronto.

2. What might happen if this person passes it on? Even if your conversation partner swears on their grandmother's grave that they will never divulge the secret to anyone else, can you really trust them? After all, someone probably trusted you, didn't they? It's worth thinking through the worst-case scenario. Who could they tell, and what might happen as a result? Remember that you never know for sure who is friends with who. You may assume that the other person doesn't know the person whose secrets you are about to divulge, whereas in reality they are close. Their loyalty might mean that things get ugly very quickly.

3. Do I even know whether this information is true? If you are going to pass on information that might change someone else's reputation – for better or for worse – make sure that you know it to be true. If you heard it from the primary source, you probably have an accurate insight into the situation. Or do you? Remember, everything can and does change. Your colleague might have told you, in confidence, that they are 13 weeks pregnant – but then had a miscarriage a few days following your conversation.

How would you feel if you discovered that you were the subject of very personal gossip? Of course, if you are simply going to invent rumors, you need to do some serious soul-searching. Once you have graduated elementary school, there is no excuse for this kind of behavior.

4. What positive or uplifting messages could I pass on instead? When I think about the worst gossips I ever met, I don't think that most of them actually meant to cause any harm. So why did they like talking about other people? For much the same reason that people love talking about the latest reality TV show – it provides them with a topic of conversation. Back in college, I used to take a history class with a girl named Laura. We'd occasionally have coffee together just after class let out. Within a few weeks of knowing her, I realized that she seized upon any opportunity to speculate about the personal lives of our classmates, our professors, and even the janitor!

She was especially eager to tell me all about the time she'd seen one of our professors walking to his car late one evening with a much younger woman. I probably spent about two hours in total listening to her ramble on about how terrible he was for cheating on his wife. Of course, she was making assumptions. She had never seen him hold hands with this woman, or even kiss her on the cheek. Laura only shut up about it when she happened to see the professor at a college recital. He was there with his wife and the "other woman," who just so happened to be his daughter. It turned out that she was taking an evening class at the school.

On reflection, Laura never had anything positive to say about anyone. I think her gossip served as filler, a way of guarding against any periods of silence. (Incidentally, you don't need to talk all the time – it's fine to have a pause here and there!) If you have a habit of talking about other people behind their backs, ask yourself when you last had a positive, uplifting conversation about something other than everyone else's dirty secrets. What other interests do you have? Do you ever feel compelled to pass on good news? Perhaps you have the same old negative conversations over and over again with the same people? If so, you need to revise your conversation habits. Stick to positive or neutral topics. There are literally thousands of other things to talk about. If you don't have a hobby, get one! Stop subjecting people to your mindless gossip, and instead form constructive relationships based on intimacy and authenticity.

In summary, knowing when to keep your mouth shut is one of the key skills you must master in order to build great relationships. The golden rule here is that if in doubt, don't keep talking. Unless the situation is life or death, err on the side of caution. Don't risk your reputation and relationships for the sake of a few pieces of gossip.

Chapter 7: Conversations That Revive Relationships

Reconnecting After A Fight

I wrote this book to help people have better conversations with everyone – friends, colleagues, and relatives. But what if there's a barrier between you and the person you want to talk to? Sadly, arguments between friends and relatives are all too common. Before you know it, the months and years have flown by, and you start to miss them. You start to wonder, "Do I get back in touch? How can I reach out and repair the relationship?"

This is where a lot of people hit a block. It's an awkward situation – what should you say, and how should you say it? In this chapter, I'll teach you how to have conversations that get a relationship back on track. Even if you stopped talking after a full-scale row, there's always a chance to revive your friendship.

Whether your argument was two weeks or two decades ago, follow these steps:

Step 1 - Check your attitude: First, make sure that you are psychologically ready to let go of the past. If you are going to make a sincere attempt at reconciliation, you cannot harbor lingering resentment or fantasies of revenge. Neither should you expect the other person to "see the light" and admit that they were the one in the wrong. The key question is this: Are you willing to value their friendship over your need to be right? Only when the answer is, "Yes, definitely," should you try to repair the relationship. Otherwise, there's a high chance that you'll start fighting over the same issue. This doesn't mean that you can't talk about the past, but it does mean that you should be prepared to let the matter lie (forever) if you can't reach an agreement.

Step 2 - Set up a call or meeting with an "I've realized" email: As a rule, I always value face-to-face interaction or phone conversations over emails. However, email (or even letters!) is the perfect tool for setting up a reconciliation. Why? Imagine yourself in the following scenario:

You have had an ugly row with a friend, and resolved never to speak to them again. A few months go by, and you're busy getting on with your life. The phone rings. You pick it up, only to hear this person's voice. Coming out of the blue, it's unnerving. It also places you on the spot – you are under pressure to make up your mind, in that very moment, as to whether or not you want to talk to this person. Even if you see their name on your phone's screen and choose to ignore it, you still have to make a choice – do you want to call them back, or ignore them? If you do call them back, you'll need to think about what you are going to say. If you don't call them back, you'll probably worry that they will call again! In any event, a burden has been placed on your shoulders.

Now, consider this alternative chain of events: One day, you receive an email or letter from your estranged friend. Within a couple of paragraphs, they explain why they are getting back in touch, tell you that they would like to meet (or talk on the phone, if distance makes meeting impossible), and that they hope you will reply. You can read and reread the email at your leisure. You can take a few days to digest it, and reply – or not. Either way, you don't have to sustain an awkward phone call with someone! You can also keep a copy, which could come in useful if you want or need to talk about this relationship with a third party at a later date.

At this point, you'll be wondering what to put in an email to an estranged friend. There are no magic words, but there is a phrase that sets the right tone. That phrase is, "I've realized." Acclaimed mediator Dr. Tammy Lenski recommends that your message should include a brief summary of the things you've realized or learned during the time you have been apart. This makes you appear thoughtful and sincere, but not overly negative. It doesn't demand answers from the other person, which means they won't feel threatened. End the email by saying that you'd like to call or meet, and hope that they'd be willing to work with you to set something up.[25] The ball is then in their court.

Obviously, you will have to tailor your email to your specific situation and personality, but here's generic example:

---

[25] Lenski, M. (2016). *How to Email Someone After a Falling Out.* Mediate.com

Dear [Their Name],

I have been thinking of you recently, and how the silence between us has made me realize a few things. I wanted to get in touch and tell you about them.

I've realized that my friendships are one of the most important things in my life, and that I don't want to let the past come between me and one of my oldest pals.

I've realized that sometimes, it's hard for me to work out problems in my friendships, but that I want to be your friend again.

Thank you for opening my email. I'd love the chance to speak to you/meet up with you. Could we set something up?

[Your Name]

There is a chance that they might not reply. Make sure that you are prepared for this outcome before making contact, and be willing to let it go if you receive no response.

Step 3 – Meet up and talk. If either of you need to clear the air, raise the issue early in the conversation: In an ideal world, both of you would be able to move on from whatever happened between you. Sometimes, especially if you fell out for a trivial reason, that's exactly how the situation can unfold. However, we don't live in an ideal world, and sometimes we must openly address what happened in the past. Otherwise, the underlying issue will continue to simmer until you have yet another fight.

This kind of conversation demands strong listening and conflict resolution skills. Remember, your aim is not to "win," but to have a constructive talk that allows both of you to feel heard. You don't have to agree with every comment they make. Aim to empathize, rather than to impose your opinions. If their interpretation of events upsets you, tell yourself that at least you know where you stand. It's your choice to either walk away, or to rekindle the relationship under a new set of terms and conditions. For example, if you and your friend fell out because you disagreed on a political matter, they might say that they are happy to be friends again – under the condition that you never again discuss heavy political topics. Be prepared to adjust your view of events as the conversation progresses. If you realize that you caused more hurt than you imagined, swallow your pride and apologize for your actions.

Step 4 – Treat them like anyone else: Once you have moved past any initial negotiations and apologies, move the conversation back to the same kinds of topics you used to talk about prior to your big argument. If it's been months or years since you last saw the other person, refer to the section below for further guidance.

What If You Just Drifted Apart?

What if you didn't fall out with a friend, but just drifted apart instead? This often happens between college friends after graduation, or between two work buddies who go on to work for different companies. If there's no animosity between you, skip the email and go straight to a phone call. Of course, if you don't have their number, an email or message on social media is fine. Tell them that you would like to hang out and catch up, or if that's not possible (for example, if they live far away), to schedule a phone call to share what has been happening in your lives.

When talking to someone who hasn't been in your life for a long time, follow these tips:

Acknowledge that it's been a long time since you last spoke: Don't try and pretend that it's been ten minutes since you last spent time together – this will make you appear a bit odd! Pair a comment about how long it's been since you last saw one another with a positive statement. For example, "It's been years! You're looking great, you always had style!" would be a good opener.

Harness nostalgia: I don't believe in dwelling on the past, but if you have a shared history that makes both of you smile, there's nothing wrong with a few references to the good old days. A bit of nostalgia will remind you of what you have in common, and will trigger old feelings of intimacy and familiarity.

Ask about mutual contacts and old acquaintances: Ask the other person whether they have been in contact with any mutual friends. This can be a fertile topic of conversation, and can help you reconnect with other people from your past.

Talk about dreams and goals: If your old friend has met their personal or professional goals, they will be happy to tell you about them, and this can be a good basis for an interesting conversation that gives you an insight into their life. However, asking, "So, did you achieve X?" can be awkward if they have failed to achieve a goal. A subtler approach is to ask them about their hopes and dreams for the future. This will usually develop naturally into a conversation that allows them the chance to bring up their past achievements. If appropriate, you can then say, "Of course, you always wanted to do X, and I'm so glad you succeeded!"

Move to the present tense: If you want to be a part of their life as it currently stands, ask them about it! You can always fall back on common topics (for example, family and hobbies) if the conversation isn't flowing naturally.

Close with a concrete suggestion or invitation: If you want to keep the flame of friendship alight, end the conversation by inviting them to an event or arranging another catch up session. Note that you should only do this if you truly want the relationship to continue. You might spend time with this person and discover that although you still like them, your lives are now so different that a regular friendship probably isn't an option. However, you will at least have enjoyed a good conversation, and that in itself is a positive outcome.

How To Maintain A Long-Distance Relationship

The phrase "long-distance relationship" conjures up the image of two lovers kept apart by circumstances beyond their control. However, most of us living in the 21st century have at least a couple of long-distance platonic or familial relationships. In days gone by, people tended to live in the same place for much of their lives, so maintaining relationships was quite straightforward. In an age where it's considered normal to move to a new state or country, you can expect to be in at least one long-distance friendship or family relationship at some point.

If you learn that your friend (or even your partner) is about to move hours away, don't give up! It's possible to maintain a close relationship even if years go by with no face-to-face communication.[26]

Use The Maintenance Behavior Model To Keep Your Relationship Strong

As you might imagine, psychologists are interested in how we conduct our relationships – including relationships carried out from afar. One of the models I really like is the Maintenance Behavior (MB) Model. This model is backed up by research that shows the best long-distance relationships are those that incorporate seven different types of maintenance behaviors.[27] Check that you've got each one covered, and your bond will remain strong!

1. Assurances: Don't assume that the other person knows how much you appreciate them. Let them know that you enjoy talking to them, and assure them that you are grateful your relationship is still intact. Insecurity is a common problem in long-distance relationships, because one or both people may start thinking, "We are only talking via a computer or phone – wouldn't they rather be out having fun in the real world?" Regular assurance can stop insecurity setting in.

2. Openness: As with all relationships, a degree of openness is needed. Telling someone about your problems and innermost thoughts is a reliable way of maintaining intimacy. However, openness also takes on extra meaning in a long-distance relationship. It means that you need to be open when the distance is affecting you – for example, if you feel as though the two of you aren't talking enough – and how to overcome your problems. Don't panic if the other person tells you that they are finding the distance hard. Empathize, and then suggest ways of overcoming the issue. For instance, if they feel as though they are no longer an important part of your life, suggest that you hold a weekly session in which you both make a point of telling the other about everything that happened over the past few days. There is no magic rule that specifies how often you have to talk to one another – it must be negotiated on a case-by-case

[26] Parrenas, R. (2005). Long distance intimacy: Class, gender and intergenerational relations between mothers and children in Filipino transnational families. *Global Networks, 5, 4,* 317-336.

[27] Stafford, L., Dainton, M., & Haas, S. (2000). Measuring routine and strategic relational maintenance: Scale revision, sex versus gender roles, and the prediction of relational characteristics. *Communication Monographs, 67, 3,* 306-323.

basis. I'd argue that quality is more important than quantity, but then again, I place a high value on efficiency! If you prefer to spend twenty minutes per day in conversation rather than talk in depth for an hour or two once a week, for example, then that's fine – as long as it works for both of you. You will need to be open in stating your preferences. You should also be prepared to be flexible. For example, someone might not have as much time to spare during the holiday season.

3. *Conflict management:* **If you have a relationship problem and you live far apart, make it a rule that you will only resolve your differences over Skype, not via text messages or the phone.** Two people need to see one another's body language to really understand what the other party is thinking or feeling. Text and even phone calls let you hide your true emotions, which can lead to conflicts going unresolved. Your negative feelings will fester over time if you don't sort out your problems when they first arise. This will cause significant damage to your relationship.

4. *Sharing tasks and activities:* In a traditional relationship, two people usually engage in real-time activities, such as going out for dinner or spending time at the park. These activities build mutual experiences and a shared history. If you are far apart, the traditional approach won't work. So what can you do instead? Find some online substitutes! You could play games together online, stream the same movie together, write a short story or poem using an online document, and even eat your meals together whilst keeping your webcams on. Shared activities allow you both to focus on something other than the conversation, which will help you both relax rather than analyze whether you are talking about sufficiently interesting topics.

5. *Positivity:* Everyone appreciates positivity in their relationships, but it's particularly vital in long-distance relationships. It's depressing to think that you might not see someone for months or years, so positivity is key in making you both feel better. Start and close every conversation on a positive note. From time to time, tell them the positive impact they have on your life. You could even try to find the upsides of long-distance relationships. For example, the feeling you get when meeting up after months or years apart is bound to be particularly special. Suggest that you both note down three positive things that happen to you each day, and then share them during your next conversation.

6. Giving advice: When you are far apart from someone, you may feel removed from their life. Sharing problems and offering advice (if the other person wants it, of course) can go some way to compensate for this gap. It will help both people feel more involved in each other's offline lives.

7. Drawing on social networks to support the relationship: Don't feel as though you have to bottle up your feelings. If you really miss the other person and the distance is getting you down, call on your other friends and relatives for support. Encourage the other person to do the same. You can also invite mutual friends to hang out online (for example, by taking part in an online game). This will allow your relationship to exist in a broader context, rather than in a little online bubble.

Keeping a relationship alive over a distance can be tough, but it can also be rewarding. **Choose video calling or the phone instead of emails and texts if possible, because this will make your conversations feel more intimate.** Video calling is ideal, because you get to see the other person's body language as well as hear their voice. Don't forget that gifts and letters still have their place. Receiving a handwritten note in the mail can make someone feel special, so make the effort to send them once in a while.

If you start to feel as though your relationship is somewhat lacking, refer back to this model. Are there any areas that you've been neglecting recently? If the other person is interested in psychology, you could even share this model with them! Working together to build a great relationship is well worth the effort.

Chapter 8: Do You Feel "Different?" How To Overcome Outsider Syndrome

So many of my clients – even those who appear pretty confident – have told me that they feel "different" or "odd" when they are around other people. My theory is that this feeling – known in self-development circles as "Outsider Syndrome" – is much more common than you might think. At some point in your life, you are going to feel like the odd one out. Perhaps you don't have much in common with your colleagues, or maybe you're in a class full of people who have known one another for years.

I'm frequently asked how to fit in as the new guy or girl in the office, or how to make friends with people who are already in established groups in the workplace. Most people can cope with feeling like an outsider for a while, but it soon becomes draining. Even for the most introverted among us, social interaction is a basic human need. In fact, regular social contact is important for our mental health – psychologists have long known that isolation increases our risk of both mental and physical illness.[28] So how can you establish yourself as a member of the in-group?

If you have a disdain for small talk, get over it: If you spend a lot of time alone, other people will assume that you dislike social interaction. They may also wonder whether they have done anything to offend you! This can lay the foundation for a vicious cycle. It goes like this: You feel like an outsider, so you don't want to approach them. They continue to leave you alone, and everyone gets used to this division – it becomes "How things are." It therefore becomes even harder to try and make friends with those in the group...and the pattern continues.

Luckily, you can break the cycle. The first step is to start sending out normality signals. These signals should communicate, "I am a social being. I would be open to talking with you." What's the ultimate normality sign? Small talk, of course! When you can look someone in the eye, ask them how their weekend went, and express interest in their health, you are sending a clear signal – "I understand the basic rules of social interaction." Remember, other people know nothing (or very little) about you if you have taken on the role as outsider. Before committing

---

[28] House, J.S., Landis, K.R., & Umberson, D. (1988). Social Relationships and Health. *Science, 241, 4865,* 540-545.

to further social interaction, they will want to satisfy themselves that you pose no danger, and that you are friendly.

There are many differences between socially successful people and those who struggle to make friends. One key factor is their perception of small talk. I've worked with at least a dozen clients who have told me stories that go along these lines:

"I just feel different. I don't think I'm better than anyone else, but I'm not like them. People are so dramatic! And all they do is talk about stupid stuff. I don't like small talk, and I don't share any of their interests. How am I supposed to make friends at work/network/get on with my partner's family?"

I always tell them that, contrary to what some people would have you believe, mastering the art of small talk doesn't make you look like a suck-up, and neither does it make you someone who is bound by the shackles of convention. The truth is that casual conversation is the bedrock of everyday interaction, and those who don't engage in it at are a serious disadvantage. This isn't just my opinion – there is plenty of academic research out there to back it up! For example, linguist Janet Holmes has spent hours in various workplaces, monitoring the ways in which people interact.[29] Her research, and that of other people, shows that if you want to make friends and influence people (as the classic saying goes), you need to be happy talking about the "little stuff." Small talk breaks down barriers.

This type of client tends to say things like, "But I never had to go through the small talk stage with my best friend! We just got on well immediately. We just clicked." Fair enough. But most friendships are first forged in the fire of casual interaction, and most co-worker relationships hinge on seemingly trivial chitchat. You are not too good for small talk, however smart or special you may feel.

If you think small talk is banal and pointless, you're missing a trick. **Small talk isn't really about exchanging information. It's about reassuring one another that you**

---

[29] Holmes, J. (2005). When small talk is a big deal: Sociolinguistic challenges in the workplace. In M.H. Long (Ed.), *Second Language Needs Analysis*, pp. 344-372. Cambridge: Cambridge University Press.

are both functional human beings who can hold a conversation. It's not enough to talk to someone once or twice, either. You are going to have to make a sustained effort. I'm talking weeks here, not a couple of days. Chat to people in the coffee room, talk to them immediately before or after a meeting, strike up small talk whilst waiting for the same bus – seize any opportunity. You might be brushed off at first, or perhaps the conversation won't last for more than ten seconds. That's OK! Persistence is key. You'll soon see the rewards – you'll develop better relationships with your colleagues, and there will be less tension at work.[30]

If you are stumped as to where to start, listen in on other people's conversations. You'll soon realize that most small talk revolves around the state of someone's well-being (e.g. "How are you?"), references to everyday events (e.g. "That meeting went on a long time, didn't it!" or "We had a lot of rain this morning!"), or compliments ("That's a really nice hat!"). Sometimes you might hear petty complaints ("Urgh, overtime again!") or clichés ("No rest for the wicked, eh?"). They all have their place. Think of small talk as a means of harmonizing with another person. It really isn't about what you are saying. It's about establishing a shared sense of trust and communication. Once you get to know someone, feel free to admit that you don't much care for small talk. You might discover that they feel the same way!

Read around, and make the most of your knowledge: Communication guru Leil Lowndes was right when she wrote that we should all be, in her words, "Renaissance men and women."[31] What does this mean? Basically, make a point of reading widely, so that you are able to jump into conversations on many different topics. Obviously, you can't hope to become an expert in every field, but you can certainly give yourself a better chance at fitting in with practically any crowd by reading new books, magazines, websites, and so on. When you have a solid grounding in many subjects, you'll feel more confident when someone asks you for an opinion, and you will feel confident in carrying on a conversation.

Skim a couple of articles on random topics every day, and you'll soon be able to contribute to even the most obscure of conversations. Pick a couple of interesting blogs that cover a variety of topics, and follow them. Don't worry about keeping up with everything that's

---

[30] Ibid.
[31] Lowndes, L. (1999). *How To Talk To Anyone*. Glasgow: Omnia Books Ltd.

going on in the world. You just need the gist of major world events, and you'll pick that up by spending a few minutes per day on Facebook. If something of earth-shattering significance happens then by all means read a news site. However, as a rule, I recommend avoiding mainstream news media. It is built on a foundation of negativity, and it will drag you down. Not only that, but your negativity will come across in the conversations you have with others. This will not help you build constructive relationships!

When talking to people you don't know, never exclaim that you find a particular subject to be trivial or stupid. You never know who might have cause to feel offended. If you want to earn your place in a group, you need to show a nonjudgmental attitude. Once you have established a few friendships, you can afford to become a bit more opinionated.

If you don't have the background knowledge necessary to take part in a conversation, get curious: What if you are in a room of people who are experts on an obscure topic or technical area, and their conversations leave you feeling out in the cold? Fall back on sincere questions. Admit that you don't have a clue what they are talking about, but make it clear that you are willing to learn. For example, if you are the only English Literature graduate in a room of statisticians, try something like, "I've heard a lot of people in here talk about loglinear modeling. It sounds pretty impressive – what exactly does that phrase mean?" Unless the person you are talking to is a complete jerk, they will gladly take the opportunity to either pass on their knowledge, or at least steer the conversation to another topic if they would rather talk about something else.

Don't be self-deprecating: Ironically, taking the time to explain how weird you are will actually make you look even stranger. Think about it. Suppose you just met someone who seems perfectly nice and normal. Suddenly they say, "I'm pretty weird! I don't have any friends, I don't think I have anything in common with you, and I've always felt out of place." Would you want to stay in the same room as that person? Probably not. Don't share your inner turmoil with people you don't know well. Save that for your therapist.

I used to make this mistake in college. If someone ever asked what I enjoyed doing in my leisure time, I'd answer with, "Ha ha, I'm pretty boring really!" or "Nothing that would interest you, just random weird stuff." Looking back, I want to cringe. If only I had actually answered those kinds of questions and tried to keep a conversation going, I might have managed to make a few more friends. You have as much value as anyone else in the room, so conduct yourself accordingly.

Intervene directly: If you are feeling bold, wait for a natural lull in the conversation and then simply establish yourself as a participant. For example, suppose you are in the breakroom at work, and three of your co-workers are discussing their vacation plans. You aren't in their social group, and you feel like an outsider. Suddenly, you hear one of them mention their love of San Francisco, which just so happens to be the city in which you grew up. You could say something like, "Excuse me, did I hear you talk about San Fran? That's where I grew up! I'd love to know what you like about it." People will be thrown off guard by this maneuver, but they'll soon get over it.

Establish in-jokes: One of the quickest ways to build rapport and lay the foundations for a relationship is to not only share a joke, but to establish a shared frame of reference. In-jokes should come naturally, so this tactic relies on an element of luck.

For example, let's say that you're talking with a colleague in the office about a recent memo circulated around the company. Suddenly, the power goes out for a few seconds. This kind of incident provides you both with a shared experience, which can become a point of reference in future conversations. During your next conversation on work-related matters, you could make a quip like, "It's nice to be able to see who you're talking to, isn't it?" This kind of remark isn't hilarious, but it shows that you are friendly, approachable, and have a sense of humor. Establishing a positive reputation for yourself will encourage other people to interact with you not just for the sake of business, but also with the intention of becoming your friend.

Sneak "we," "we're," and "us" in a few times: "We," "we're," and "us" might be small words, but they are mighty. When you talk to your close friends and family, you probably use them a lot – "When we go to Grandma's for Christmas, we'll have a great time," "We're looking forward to trying out that new restaurant in town," and so on. These phrases imply intimacy and shared experienced.

You can use them with people you don't know very well to imply that you are similar. This tactic works particularly well in the workplace, because you are all part of the same system and share the same objectives. Consider the difference "we," "we're," or "us" makes to the following sentences:

"From what I understand, this project needs to be done by July."
"It looks like *we're* going to have to get this project done by July."

"Did you see that email from the boss? Everyone has to attend the Monday meeting."
"Did you get that email the boss sent *us? We* need to attend the Monday meeting."

Over time, these small words create an impression of solidarity. They signal that you and the other person are on the same team. They will feel more inclined to think that the two of you are alike – and therefore, they will begin to feel more comfortable around you. After all, it's natural to talk to someone who is similar to you.

Set up a conversation bridge: This works in much the same way as the in-joke technique described above, but it doesn't rely on chance happenings or humor. If you are talking to someone you'd like to get to know, set up a conversation starter you can use later. When it seems as though the conversation is coming to a close, wrap up by asking the other person to explain a particular idea to you another time, or tell them that you look forward to hearing the full story behind an event they have already referenced. Ideally, this should relate to something the other person (or group) feels really passionate about. The next time the two of you talk, you can steer the conversation back to the topic in question. This sets the stage for a positive interaction that will help develop your relationship.

An example will show you how well this trick can help forge a relationship. I used to work with a pretty grumpy guy. I'll call him Sam. Sam had a tendency to either get on really well with people in the office, or to shut them out. There was no middle ground with him – you were either his buddy, or on the receiving end of icy politeness. For the first couple of months after joining the company, I was definitely on his "out" list. Unfortunately, given that he occupied a senior position in my department, I couldn't afford to ignore him. I knew I'd have to employ my best conversation skills if I was to build any sort of relationship with Sam.

One morning, we were both standing by the water cooler. The tap was broken, and no water was coming out. "Damn!" he exclaimed. "This thing is useless. I might as well be in the Sahara again!" I didn't understand his reference to the desert. I was so puzzled that I found myself saying aloud, "You've been to the Sahara?" Sam laughed and said, "Yes, I've been to the Sahara, and some other seriously exotic places! Not that you'd guess by looking at me." I told him that I looked forward to hearing all about it over lunch sometime. He looked confused, but not annoyed. He muttered something under his breath, and returned to his desk.

Later that week, when getting lunch in the canteen, I realized that I was standing behind Sam in the queue. After we paid for our food, I asked whether we could eat together. Before he could object, I told him that I was serious when I said I wanted to hear the Sahara story. He looked stunned for a few seconds, but we went on to have a great conversation about his adventures. It turned out that he was a veteran traveler who loved exploring remote places. He had journeyed all over the world in his college days, and had many tales to tell. That lunch was the start of a friendship that continues to this day. Not only did I get to know Sam, but he made a point of introducing me to several other people in the department.

If you want to get acquainted with a group at work, look for the leader: As my story with Sam illustrates, striking up a rapport with a socially influential individual can be your gateway to further introductions. If you want to earn membership to a particular group, watch them in action. **You'll soon notice who holds the most power. Whilst it's best to try and build rapport with as many people as possible, the group leader is the one you really need to impress.** If you can find some kind of common ground or just engage in small talk a few times each week, you can gradually build a meaningful relationship that will make your working life a lot easier.

Being an outsider can be an uncomfortable feeling, especially if you are an extrovert who loves to be part of a group. Luckily, it only takes a few little tricks to endear yourself to most people. At the same time, I want to end this section on a cautionary note. Sometimes, it really isn't in your best interests to try and join a particular group. Occasionally, you'll come across a clique so toxic that the company they can provide comes at too high a price. If your attempts to get to know someone get thrown back in your face, along with a side helping of intimidation or even bullying, stop with the masochism. Don't waste your valuable time on people who don't deserve it.

Chapter 9: Avoiding Excessive Negativity In Your Social Interactions

What's the most serious mistake most people make when talking to others? In my experience, both in my personal life and in talking with my clients, the quickest way to kill your social life is to infuse all your conversations with negativity. I'm not going to suggest that everyone should always adopt a Pollyanna attitude – that would get old pretty quick. But what you need to understand is that grumbling, griping, and generally spreading negativity isn't going to win you any friends. Obvious, right? Sadly, it doesn't seem obvious to lots of people out there. In fact, some of the most negative people I've ever met seem totally oblivious to their own depressing conversation habits.

Negative Conversation Habits You Need To Kick

So how do you start combating the negativity habit? The below is a list of the most common mistakes I see in ordinary day-to-day scenarios. When you pay attention to your own conversations and those of others around you, you'll be alarmed by how often they come up!

Starting every conversation with a complaint: Have you ever asked someone how they are, only to be met with an answer along the lines of, "Yeah OK I guess, too much work to do, and the weather isn't great, but…"? How does it make you feel? Negative answers to innocent conversation openers are not a good way to open a social interaction. Even if you have a legitimate complaint, try not to make your first response completely negative. For example, if you have a headache, open with something like, "I'm doing OK, just got a bit of a headache!" This gives the other person an accurate insight into how you are doing, but doesn't make you seem too downbeat and pessimistic.

Saying things that will earn you a reputation as a whiny, soul-destroying individual: How can I put this? If you suspect that you need to cut down on the amount of time you spend complaining about your life, you should probably follow your gut. Set yourself a challenge. **The next time you have a conversation of any appreciable length (say, more than ten minutes), count how many times you whine or complain. You might be shocked!**

The problem with being a chronic complainer is that you don't just poison one particular conversation. You also risk developing a negative reputation that will shape how other people interact with you. Remember, if you are building a relationship with someone, no conversation happens in isolation. It's OK to vent a little every now and then, but after a few negative conversations, people will start to suspect that you harbor a toxic personality. As a result, they will start to avoid you. Whenever you are about to start complaining or dumping your problems onto your conversation partner, take a moment to reflect on how your behavior will affect your reputation.

Shutting down upbeat comments or perspectives: The best conversationalists take into account the feelings and moods of other people. We've all had days when everything seems to go wrong – the car won't start, we argue with our partner, we lose our phone, and so on – and then we run into someone who seems so darn happy! This kind of situation is grating, even though we know that it isn't their fault that we are having a bad day. It's tempting to pass on your bad mood and shut down someone else's happiness into the bargain.

What do the most socially successful people do in this kind of situation? They spot an opportunity to ride the wave of someone else's happy mood, and use it to make both parties feel good. For example, suppose someone had a hellish journey into work one morning, and then became drawn into a conversation with a very upbeat, smiley colleague. They could give brusque responses, grumble about their journey, and ruin both their own mood and that of their co-worker.

On the other hand, they could say something like "Well I had a pretty bad commute this morning, but I'm here now, and it's great to see someone looking so happy!" This type of remark sets the stage for a much more positive interaction. Not only would both people in this situation enjoy the conversation, but the unfortunate commuter would grow their reputation as someone who took inconveniences in their stride. That's a good reputation to have.

Interjecting with a negative opinion for no good reason: We all have our own opinions, which is fine – but there's no reason to tell everyone that you disagree with someone else's ideas unless there is a sound reason for you to do so. Saying things like, "I don't agree," or "I don't like that" is not going to endear you to anyone. All it does is lower the tone of the conversation and possibly make other people feel uncomfortable. If there are some confrontational people in the room, you even risk triggering an unnecessary argument.

Giving pessimistic predictions that aren't based on solid evidence: It's always a good idea to remain realistic. I've got no problem with anyone who outlines the potential problems with an idea, if they really want to offer their help. What annoys me – and what annoys a lot of other people – is someone who seems intent on projecting a bleak outcome just for the sake of it. Some people seem to get a weird rush out of playing the role of prophet. If this sounds like you, find another means of channeling your desire for drama. Before pronouncing that the end is nigh, ask yourself, "Do I really have any evidence for this prediction?" If you do, present it in a clear, logical manner. If you don't, hold your tongue.

Pedantry: Sometimes, pointing out other people's mistakes is helpful. More often than not, it's irritating. Unless someone makes a serious error, just let it go. After all, wouldn't you want others to extend you the same courtesy?

Forgetting where you are: Not all conversation "rules" are applicable to every situation. I'm sure, as you've gone through this book, you've thought, "Well, that doesn't always apply to me!" or "I don't need to think about this when I talk to my friends!" It's a fair point – I can only give you general guidelines to follow.

However, it's important to remember that every social group has its own conventions when it comes to how you express yourself, and this includes the degree of negativity you can get away with. For example, if your closest friends enjoy making dark jokes or complaining about their everyday problems, then go ahead and do the same! The trick is to remember where you are. If in doubt, err on the side of positivity. Bear in mind that if you tend to hang around with people who are comfortable with negativity, you need to check yourself when talking to more mainstream folk.

Diminishing other people's experiences by one-upping them: If you've ever witnessed a game of one-upmanship (and who hasn't?) between two or more people, you'll know how destructive this habit is. It's fine to share good news with others, but subjecting them to long monologues about how much better you are than everyone else in the room is a sign of a narcissist – and who wants that kind of reputation?[32]

A few months ago, I was at a large family party. The atmosphere was great, and it was wonderful to catch up with relatives I don't often see. I was standing around with two of my cousins, having a couple of drinks, when a guy I didn't know came over to join us. I'll call him Rob. Rob, who turned out to be my female cousin's date, wasted no time in telling us all about his plans for the winter break. These plans just so happened to center around three weeks of skiing at one of Europe's most expensive resorts. We listened politely. Finally, he slowed down a little and asked us whether we ever went skiing. I told him that I'd been a couple of times, but preferred snowboarding. My cousin Mike said that although he hadn't been skiing, he had been on a couple of snowmobiling trips.

Anyone would think that Rob was an expert in every winter sport on the planet. He didn't want to listen to our experiences. Everything we said was just an excuse for him to engage in some serious one-upmanship. He talked at length about his snowboarding experiences, his snowmobiling experiences, and how his ski instructor had hinted he had the potential to compete at a professional level. He'd been to every resort worth visiting, he'd tried every sport worth trying, and his equipment was (obviously) much more expensive than ours. I wanted to intervene and shut the conversation down but, at the same time, I found his sheer arrogance quite fascinating. Needless to say, we all breathed a sigh of relief when my cousin showed up and told him that it was time to leave. Incidentally, she dumped him a few weeks later. I don't know the full story, but I have the feeling that his conversation skills (or lack thereof) had something to do with it.

Don't be like Rob. By all means share your experiences if you get the chance, but never try to outdo your conversation partner. You'll look like a jerk, and who wants to be known as a show-off? **No one will want to open up to you in the future, because they'll just assume that you will attempt to show just how much "better" you are.**

---

[32] Mills, C. (2003). Bragging, Boasting, and Crowing: The Ethics Of Sharing One's Glad Tidings With Others. *Philosophy & Public Policy Quarterly, 23, 4,* 7-12.

Expecting someone else to do all the work: Some people, perhaps due to shyness or laziness, like to sit back and shove the responsibility for keeping the conversation going onto someone else. This is totally unacceptable. It suggests to the other person that you don't consider them sufficiently interesting to merit any effort on your part. You are inviting them to perform for your own entertainment. Step up and take on your fair share! Pay attention to what they are saying. **Ask questions, and give thoughtful responses when they want you to provide more information.** If you can't be bothered to meet someone halfway, excuse yourself from the situation rather than force them to keep a one-sided interaction going.

Oversharing, or telling people too much about your problems: Have you ever met someone who felt compelled to open up about their most personal problems within ten minutes? How did it make you feel? In all probability, they came off as insecure and lacking in boundaries. Letting all the skeletons out of the closet at the very start of a relationship creates a false sense of intimacy. It places pressure on the other person to either listen to your problems and put together a sensitive response, or disclose their own trials and tribulations (which may make them feel very uncomfortable). Keep your first few conversations light. If you become friends with a new acquaintance, there will be plenty of time for sharing your grisly secrets later.

Questioning someone else's life choices: When it comes to childrearing, dietary practices, religion, and other potentially sensitive life choices, keep quiet. Unless you have been asked for your opinion, you should never, ever, ask someone to justify how they choose to live their personal life. Things often start to get ugly pretty quickly if you pursue these avenues. Even if your conversation partner happens to be a close friend, you need to read the situation carefully. If in doubt, ask whether they would mind if you asked them a sincere question on the matter. If they seem at all reluctant, say that you understand their reticence and then change the subject.

Allowing a negative conversation to continue for too long: You might not have taken a conversation in a negative direction, but you can choose to turn it around or draw it to a close. Don't waste your time.

Repeating yourself to the point of becoming patronizing: Not everyone will be receptive to the points you are making. Sometimes, you might need to explain a point again from another angle. However, if you find yourself taking on the role of "teacher," patronizing your "student" and making the same point over and over again – stop! Unless it's absolutely crucial that the other person understands what you are talking about, just let it go. Don't set up an imbalanced power dynamic. If you are both adults, a conversation should be an exchange between equals. Do not talk down to anyone. If someone isn't able to understand you, maybe it's time to consider whether you are explaining it properly in the first place. Never assume that the problem always lies with somebody else.

Reminiscing about the good old days with someone who is going through a rough patch: Resist the temptation to talk about how someone used to be. For example, if you are talking to a person who used to have a great job, but was then made redundant and had to take a new position that didn't come with the same salary and prestige, talking about their old role will make them feel like dirt. A more positive approach is to focus on what is going well for them right now.

Failing to keep your body language positive: However encouraging you are, the effect will be lost if your body language doesn't match your words. For example, if you are telling someone how much you enjoy your new job but sit with your shoulders slumped, they aren't going to believe you.[33]

Can Anyone Learn To Be Positive?

Absolutely. We all have the ability to learn new ways of communicating with others, and leading a more positive life in general[34]. Don't be discouraged if the list of habits above sound all too familiar. The key is to recognize that you need to change, and then to make yourself aware of your behaviors. There's no need to alter your personality, just your communication techniques. All you are doing when you decide to be positive is changing what you focus on. If you have a reputation for being somewhat grumpy, your friends and colleagues might be a little surprised to see the the transformation. However, within a few weeks, they'll be grateful that

[33] Pease, A., & Pease, B. (2016). *The Definitive Book of Body Language: How To Read Others' Attitudes By Their Gestures.* London: Hachette UK.
[34] Seligman, M.E.P., & Csikszentmihalyi, M. (2000). Positive Psychology: An Introduction. *American Psychologist, 55, 1,* 5-14.

you decided to work on yourself.

Chapter 10: The Ethical Conversationalist – Getting Your Views Across & Needs Met Without Harming Others

Great conversationalists can wield significant influence. However, some people start to feel uneasy when I talk about social influence. I've had readers ask me to write about the ethics of good conversation. How can you use your skills to build the relationships you want, whilst respecting other people? When is it acceptable to tell a lie? In this section, I'm going to tell you how to use your powers for the greater good.

Is It "Bad" To Try & Control The Behavior Of Someone Else?

If someone were to accuse you of being "controlling," you probably wouldn't take it as a compliment. Not many of us like to think that we gain satisfaction or enjoyment from dictating how other people should act. In some cases, the fear of being "too powerful" can even hold people back from developing their social skills. I had one client who asked me in our second session, "I'm a bit worried. All these techniques you're teaching me, they work! People are really starting to listen to me!" He hesitated, then continued, "I'm not sure that I'm comfortable with this. I mean, it's odd to be able to influence people." He then asked whether it's OK to deliberately change someone's mind, or even persuade them to do something that they'd previously refused to do.

In answering such questions, I like to make two points:

1. We all attempt to control one another, whether we intend to do so or not. Conversation is supposed to be about exchanging information for a purpose, and quite often that purpose is to bring about some kind of change in other people. To use a basic example, when you ask your friend to stop off at the store on the way to your house to pick up a six-pack of beer, you are (technically speaking) trying to control their behavior. When you knock on your boss's door and ask them whether they have a spare five minutes in which to talk, you are attempting to control their behavior. It's basic stuff. I think we can all agree that these situations are not in any way ethically ambiguous.

What about using conversation to try and change how someone feels and thinks? Again, many of us do this on a daily basis. For example, suppose you come home from work one day and go to greet your partner. They seem a bit tired. To cheer them up, you might tell them that you love them, and that you will make dinner even though it's their turn to cook. You are using your words to change their feelings, and there's nothing malicious in it whatsoever. To use another example, if you are telling someone that you think they should buy a particular phone because it has better specifications for a lower price than others they have been looking at, you are attempting to change the way they think.

Once you've spent a few minutes contemplating this kind of everyday example, you'll realize that benign manipulation is no big deal. When you learn to improve your conversation skills and gain the respect of others, you just get better at doing what we all do anyway. Manipulation has a bad reputation, but if you look up the definition of "manipulate," you'll learn that the word denotes the act of handling something carefully and with skill, in order to elicit a desired outcome. Provided you remain respectful of other people's basic rights, I see nothing wrong in learning a few tricks that will help you leave a powerful impression. Good conversationalists are indeed more influential and command more respect, but it's up to them to decide whether they will use their skills for better or worse. If you want a few guidelines to follow, bear these in mind:

Don't try to change someone's mind for the sake of it: Debating can be enjoyable and intellectually stimulating. Even playing devil's advocate can be fun – as long as both people are ready and willing to examine their opinions in a playful way. However, setting out to challenging someone's cherished beliefs just for the sake of proving your powers of persuasion is a waste of their time. You could potentially leave them feeling confused and upset if you have succeeded in challenging their worldview. Moreover, some people just don't like verbal combat. If you get any verbal or nonverbal signals that they aren't in the mood for debating, drop it and change the subject.

Don't attempt to play two people off against one another: There's no denying it – drama can be interesting and even kind of amusing. That's why TV shows are full of it. In the real world, however, it's completely unethical to manipulate two or more people into arguing with one another. Vicious fights can upset even the most stable of relationships. Always take on the role of peacemaker, not agitator. If you realize that a conversation is heading into dangerous territory that could culminate in an unnecessary and heated exchange of views, turn it in a safer direction.

Don't attempt to manipulate anyone who is clearly at a disadvantage: If you are talking to someone who is clearly less knowledgeable, significantly less intelligent, or much more naïve than you, make the conscious decision to play fair. For example, don't attempt to bulldoze someone into submission by bombarding them with jargon specific to your field.

Ask yourself whether your idol would admire you in any given situation: If you suspect that your behavior isn't based on positive intentions, think about whether someone you admire for their morals and integrity would behave in a similar manner. Would you act differently if you knew that they were watching? Failing that, ask yourself whether you would be able to justify your behavior to your mother or father!

Given that so many people remain in a state of blissful ignorance when it comes to their own personality and social behaviors[35], I'd argue that learning more about how conversation works and how to persuade other people of your arguments is actually a responsible act. When you know what to watch out for in yourself and others, you'll know when to press a point, when to back off, and how to make your point in the least intimidating way possible.

2. Give other people some credit. Most of us know when someone else isn't acting with our best interests in mind. Yes, some people are convincing liars and accomplished con artists, but the majority will slip up when trying to manipulate someone over a long period of time. When you set out to change someone's mind or ask them for a favor, they will probably realize what you are trying to do. It's then up to them to decide how they want to handle the situation. Yes, you are responsible for how you treat others, but they are responsible for asserting

---

[35] Chamorro-Premuzic, T. (2015). *Why You Lack Self-Awareness And What To Do About It.* fastcompany.com

themselves and taking a realistic view of any given social situation.

What About Lying & Omissions?

From an early age, we are told that deceiving someone else is a bad thing to do. However, it doesn't take long before a child realizes that adults do not tell the truth. Parents often have to answer difficult questions such as, "If you said that Aunty Susan's dress is really horrible, why did you say that it was nice when she came for lunch?" Even as adults, we end up in situations that make us wonder, "Should I have told the truth?" or "Should I keep quiet, and lie by omission?"

Lying is unethical for several reasons. First, most of us would agree that a relationship built on lies is intrinsically less "good" than one built on truth. Second, when we lie to someone, we rob them of the right to make informed decisions about their future, because they will be acting on inaccurate assumptions. Finally, as philosopher Immanuel Kant argued, the act of lying corrupts the liar.[36] When you gain a self-image as a liar, you might become content to deceive others on a regular basis. However, most of us realize that lying is sometimes necessary.

So When Is It Acceptable To Tell A Lie?

When it passes the "test of publicity:" Sissela Bok, a philosopher known for her work on the ethics of deception, states that a lie is morally acceptable if it "would survive the appeal for justification to reasonable persons." In other words, if you think that most people would agree that lying was the right thing to do, you are probably OK.[37]

When it relates to trivial matters: There's nothing wrong with lying about minor things, such as the time you left the house on your way to a meeting (e.g. "I left at five," when in fact you were running late and left at ten past).

To spare someone's feelings, particularly with regards to minor issues: If your friend

[36] Mazur, T.C. (2015). *Lying.* scu.edu
[37] BBC. (2014). *Lying and truth-telling.* bbc.co.uk

asks whether you like their new hat or car, it's probably a good idea to tell a white lie and pretend you think it's great. Telling the truth (e.g. "To be honest, I hate it!") isn't going to help anyone.

In situations in which lying is expected: For the sake of convention and harmony, most people say things like, "It was a pleasure doing business with you," "We'd love to see you again soon," and "Yes, we got your gift, and it was just what we wanted." Technically, these are often lies, but they are so firmly embedded in Western culture that we see them as not only acceptable but desirable.

Note that the act of lying is not always a straightforward endeavor. Even small social lies can come back to haunt you. For example, suppose that you attend a dinner party and the host serves you a dish that tastes unpleasant. Because he put a lot of time and effort into the party, you may tell a social lie and assure him that you love his cooking. Unfortunately, your lie might encourage him to prepare it again in the future!

A lot of people believe that it's acceptable to tell a lie if doing so will result in a more favorable outcome than *not* telling it.[38] Unfortunately, what we don't often consider is that it's hard to predict the consequences of any given situation. For example, you might feel as though it's acceptable to tell your friend that you think she is smart enough to get into medical school, even though you know that she probably isn't, just to spare her feelings. However, if she then decides to pour a lot of time and effort into studying for entrance exams only to be rejected, how would you feel? When you tell a lie, you are taking a risk. You don't know how well someone will react to the truth, but you can at least know that you have not deceived them and are giving them the right to make their own choices based on accurate information.

Another thing to consider is whether a particular lie will mushroom. The best kind of lies are small, delivered with the best of intentions, and don't require a load of other lies to prop them up. As Sir Walter Scott famously wrote, "O what a tangled web we weave when first we practice to deceive." Often, it's simpler just to tell the truth.

---

[38] Ibid.

Gossiping

Gossiping about other people is not only a quick and easy way of ruining your own reputation, but it can also damage that of another person. When you pass on rumors or speculation for the sake of entertainment, you are endangering their reputation (and risking a confrontation if they find out that you have been gossiping about them) for the sake of your own enjoyment. This just isn't ethical. Don't do it.

Humor At The Expense Of Other People

Humor is an effective tool in conversation, and it can build a great relationship between two people. You can even make jokes at the expense of other people – as long as you know for certain that someone will take it in the right spirit. For instance, if you are hanging out with your best friend, you can probably afford to make a few jokes about their quirks, or playfully remind them about embarrassing or amusing incidents from their past. However, if you aren't sure how readily someone else will take offense, it's best to stick to safer types of humor. Mocking someone who isn't laughing along with you is just plain cruel. People are not there for you to ridicule, and words can cut deep.

A client once told me that the "jokes" her father made about her "chubby bits" during her adolescence damaged her self-esteem for years. To this day, she is especially sensitive to any wisecracks about her appearance. You might not think that your remarks could have any serious effects, but you have no way of knowing whether you are poking at old wounds. If in doubt, cut the teasing and focus on positive topics instead.

Part II: Conversation Skills

Chapter 11: How To Use The FORD Method To Keep Any Conversation Alive

We've all been there. You're talking to someone, everything seems to be going well…and then the conversation shows signs of slowing down, or even stopping altogether. Luckily, there's one little acronym will save you every time.

Remember – FORD[39]

What do people enjoy talking about the most? Themselves, of course! Even the most considerate among us appreciate the chance to air our opinions and share our life experiences. When you run out of things to say, just think FORD.

F - Family

This is a universally relevant topic of conversation. After all, everyone has a family. Even if they are estranged from their relatives or have a poor relationship with them, it all counts! However, take it slow. Jumping in with a question like, "So, do you get on well with your family?" will make you seem a bit too intense. Instead, direct the conversation to the topic in such a manner that it doesn't seem forced.

You can do this by mentioning your own family. For instance, suppose you were taking a class taught by a professor who reminded you of your eccentric Uncle Andrew. You could mention this fact casually if you wanted to provide a natural bridge into a conversation about relatives. You could say, "You know, our professor really reminds me of my Uncle Andrew – they're both really fond of speaking ridiculously loudly!" This provides a natural opener for a discussion about families in general, quirky relatives, and so on.

Another way you can direct the topic to family is by mentioning a relevant news story. For example, you could say something like, "You know, there's this new study out that says elder siblings are smarter than their younger brothers and sisters." Most people would take the

---

[39] Practical Psychology. (2016). *How To Never Run Out Of Things To Say –Keep A Conversation Flowing!* https://youtu.be/vU-ibdHkz4Y

opportunity to respond in the context of their own experiences. For example, your conversation partner might say, "Well, I don't believe that! I have an older sister, but she's as dumb as a rock!" This would provide you with an opportunity to ask further questions about the number of siblings they have, why they think their sister is dumb, and so on.

Of course, you need to remember that some people have a history of family trauma,[40] and may not want to talk about the subject at all. If you get the impression they are at all uncomfortable, back off and transition to another topic. Should the two of you become friends, the subject will probably come up at a later date, and they may feel happier sharing more of their background once they feel safe around you.

O - Occupation

Almost everyone has an occupation. Asking what someone does for a living is fairly safe, because most of us have been raised to think that it is a socially appropriate question. However, don't make the mistake of asking a series of obvious questions that put someone on the spot. Whilst asking questions is a sign of interest, and is generally a good strategy, you risk entering into interrogation mode or "interview mode" if you aren't careful.

For example, let's say that you have been introduced to a woman and ask her what she does for a living. She tells you that she is a nurse. In this situation, most people would then throw a volley of questions, such as:

"Do you work with adults or children?"
"How long have you been working as a nurse?"
"Where did you go to school?"
"Do you work night shifts, day shifts, or a mixture of both?"

The trouble with this approach is that it comes across as quite intense. It's better to ask the other person what they do for a living, give a thoughtful response to their reply, and then

---

[40] Ezpleta, L. et al. (2016). Development of a screening tool enabling identification of infants and toddlers at risk of family abuse and neglect: A feasibility study from three South European countries. *Child: Care, Health and Development, 1-6.*

let the conversation develop naturally.

To continue with the nurse example, a comment such as, "Oh wow, I've always admired nurses. It looks like a really pressured job, and I guess you need to make important decisions every day," would be a good response. Quite often, you won't have to launch into interview mode if you give this kind of reply, because the other person will feel compelled to either build on what you have said, or correct you. This results in a natural conversation and better rapport.

If your conversation partner is not in work, you can take the same approach when asking about their college classes or what they like to do in their spare time. **Under no circumstances should you make clichéd jokes or remarks about someone else's occupation.** They've heard them all before, and you will only make yourself look foolish. For example, no lawyer wants to hear yet another reference to ambulance chasing, and no vet wants to hear another "joke" about killing people's pets.

R - Recreation

Aside from work or study, what does everyone do? Engage in hobbies or pursue their interests, of course! Recreation can be a conversational goldmine if you seize the opportunity. Much like jobs and college courses, recreation is an area that people expect to crop up in conversation. It's therefore acceptable to simply ask, "What do you like to do in your free time?"

Don't panic if someone mentions an obscure hobby, or an interest that doesn't appeal to you in the slightest. Admit that you know nothing about their hobby, but make it clear that you want to know more about their lives and experiences. Say something like, "Oh, I don't know much about that, but I know that people who do it tend to love it! What do you most like about it?" Even if you aren't in a position to understand what they are actually talking about, you can still build rapport by asking about their feelings.

Occasionally, you might meet someone who is too busy working to enjoy any hobbies. These people value their work above everything else – even if they don't actually like doing it –

and have few other interests in life.[41] (Resist any urge you might have to tell them that their work-life balance needs some adjustment, because they won't listen.) There are two approaches you can take when talking to a workaholic about their hobbies and interests. If they seem to enjoy their job, make that the focus of conversation instead. If not, ask them what they would like to do if they had any free time.

D - Dreams

This is probably the most personal of the four topics, but if you can hold a meaningful conversation about someone's dreams, they will feel kindly towards you. Why? Because most people harbor some kind of ambition or secret longing, but rarely get the chance to share them with someone else. Human beings want to be understood and validated. Therefore, if you can listen to someone's dreams in a nonjudgmental manner, and even encourage them to pursue them, they will think you a first-rate conversationalist!

Don't dive straight in by asking someone, "So, do you have any secret dreams or unfulfilled ambitions?" You need to take a subtler route. For example, you could use one of their hobbies or interests as a springboard, and make an educated guess as to what their dream might be. If someone mentions that they love to read contemporary fiction and write short stories, ask them whether they have ever thought of becoming a professional author. It doesn't matter whether your guess is correct, because it will move the conversation along regardless.

Another option is to move the conversation in a more existential direction.[42] Ask them a question that prompts them to think, "What's it all about?" Mention an event that made an impact on you, and tell them that sometimes you start to wonder whether you should be taking your own dreams more seriously. This usually sets up a conversation about unfulfilled ambitions. You could take a more direct approach and tell them about something on your bucket list that you plan to do later in the year. This allows you to ask a question like, "Do you have a bucket list?" If they do, ask them what's on it. If they don't, ask them what they'd most like to achieve before their time on earth is up.

---

[41] Smith, J. (2015). *Answer these 20 questions to find out if you're a workaholic.* uk.businessinsider.com
[42] Ibid.

Getting The Most From The FORD Strategy

The four FORD topics are universal. They allow you to have a conversation with anyone from young children to the elderly, and everyone in between. However, they are most powerful when you use them to probe beyond the surface, and discover what really makes someone who they are. The more you focus on feelings and meaning rather than facts, the greater the rapport, and the more meaningful the conversation. Don't worry if the conversation takes an unexpected turn of events – these topics are intended as starting points that work well as points of discussion in their own right, but can easily develop into a fascinating exchange of experiences and views. The key is to avoid bombarding someone with questions, and to maintain a fair balance by offering a similar amount of information about yourself.

Bonus Topics For Conversation

The FORD strategy gives you four broad areas you can mine for conversation, but there are a few more topics that can work to keep a dialogue going.

Current affairs: Once upon a time, people could make a choice to completely avoid the news. All they had to do was avoid newspapers and news programs. We don't really have that choice any more – major issues of the day pop up as trends on social media, and almost every lifestyle site at least touches on current affairs. This is great news for you, because it means that almost everyone you talk to will have at least a vague idea of what is happening in the world. It isn't a good idea to watch the regular news too often – there's far too much negativity in most mainstream media – but keeping up to date with the headlines will help you find common ground in conversation. Try these phrases:

"Hey, did you happen to read about….?"
"So I was reading about [insert interesting event here – preferably sometime positive]. What do you think about that?"
"[Interesting topic] is trending on Twitter/Instagram/other social media platform today, did you happen to see it?"

One word of warning – if you are going to talk about anything remotely related to politics or religion, consider your audience. Be prepared to divert the topic if it turns out that you hit upon one of their red-button issues. If you have the suspicion that whoever you are talking to holds views that are rather different from your own, it's best to stick to lighter subjects. If in doubt, talk about the weather, celebrities, movies, sporting events, or any other issue that won't generate too much controversy. Don't let the conversation degenerate into a fight.

Pets: Lots of people own pets, and those who don't often wish they did. Pet owners form strong bonds with their animals. If you've ever heard a dog owner talk for half an hour about the way Fluffy likes to sit on the couch and bark along with the radio (yes, I have had this experience), you'll know that pets can be a gateway to a lengthy conversation. You can ask someone whether they have any pets, and if so, what they are like. Other avenues to explore include pets your family owned when you were growing up, and what pets you would like to own.

Your surroundings: This works in almost any situation. Quite simply, you find something notable about the location in which you are interacting with the other person, and comment on it. For example, if you are at the beach and talking to a girl or guy you just met, you could comment on how beautiful the water looks when the sun goes down. This then provides the other person with an opportunity to agree, and add their own experiences or opinions (e.g. "Yes, although I prefer to come here in the mornings, because I like to run before work…").

Hypothetical questions: Questions that set up thought experiments can be a fun way of adding humor and creating rapport. Common variations include, "If you had to choose between X and Y, which would you pick?" and "If someone gave you the opportunity to change X, would you take it?" This type of game can allow you to get to know someone pretty quick.

Spotting the opportunities for topics is a skill that comes with practice. The first few times you use the FORD acronym or draw on the list of subjects above, you'll be conscious that you are using a specific strategy designed to improve the quality of your conversations. However, over time, it'll become second nature. You need never worry about running out of things to say ever again!

Chapter 12: The Art Of The Compliment

A good compliment can leave someone smiling for hours. If you want to be a great conversationalist, you need to learn how to give and receive them with grace and style.

What Do The Best Compliments Have In Common?

They are sincere: Never praise someone unless they deserve it. Do not give fake compliments. Those around you will realize what you are doing and, as a result, assume that you are ready and willing to manipulate people for your own ends. This hardly inspires trust.

They are given at just the right moment: Don't wait too long to deliver a compliment. The sooner it's given, the greater the impact. For example, if you have been to see your friend perform in a play, the best time to tell them how well they did is within a few minutes of the encore, not the next morning.

They should be specific: Don't leave your target wondering exactly what you meant by broad words and terms such as "smart," "organized," or "nice." Focus on specific events and behaviors. For example, "You are so nice," is wishy-washy and non-specific, whereas "You really listened to me, and it made all the difference when I was down earlier" is more powerful.

They are not given just to make the giver look good: Giving a sincere compliment will make you feel warm and fuzzy inside, and will boost your target's self-esteem. Research shows that (as you might expect), that giving a compliment will usually make someone feel more kindly towards you.[43] It might also improve your reputation in the eyes of anyone who happens to be watching. However, this should be seen as a positive side effect rather than an end in its own right. Don't try and build a reputation as someone who compliments everyone all the time. Instead, become a person who passes on genuine praise when they feel it necessary.

They usually focus primarily on character traits and actions, rather than appearance:

---

[43] Grant, N.K., Fabrigar, L.R., & Lim, H. (2010). Exploring the Efficacy of Compliments as a Tactic for Securing Compliance. *Basic and Applied Social Psychology, 32*, 226-233.

Everyone likes to feel attractive, but compliments often seem more meaningful when they hone in on someone's core characteristics and achievements. For example, "You were so kind to help me out during that tough meeting" or "That sponsored mountain climb you did was awesome, you're so brave for doing that!" often carry more weight than, "You're pretty" or "You're hot."

In short, complimenting someone's appearance is a potential minefield, and is best avoided in most situations. If you want to do it, pick out part of their outfit (e.g., "That color is great on you!") or tell them that a new accessory or hairstyle suits them. Specific comments about someone's face or body are liable to come across as creepy or offensive.

Note that there are, of course, exceptions to this rule. For example, if you are picking someone up at a party and want to make your intentions clear, it's fine to give a couple of appearance-based compliments. Girlfriends, boyfriends, and spouses also like to be reminded that their partners find them attractive. However, even when the relationship between two people allows for this kind of compliment, it should still be sincere and delivered at the right moment.

Why You Shouldn't Always Deliver Compliments In Person

Rather than complimenting someone to their face, why not do it behind their back? All you need is a third party who knows the person you want to compliment, and who can be relied upon to talk to them in the near future. When you talk to this third party, casually bring the topic round to your target. Make it clear that you admire something specific about them. For example, you might say to your co-worker, "I saw Ben give a presentation yesterday. He's such an engaging speaker!" Then, you would continue with the conversation as normal.

Sometimes the third party will forget the conversation, but more often than not they will seize the next chance to pass on the good news. If your target seems friendlier than usual towards you, there's a good chance that your "carrier" has spread the message. Sometimes, the carrier might even tell you that they passed on the compliment. You'll need to rely on luck to some extent, so don't try this strategy if you absolutely must ensure that your target learns what you think about them. However, when it works out, it makes the target feel particularly special.

They'll think that if you have been going to the trouble of telling others how great you think they are, your sentiment must be truly sincere. This approach also reduces the risk that your target will interpret your compliment as a naked attempt to get on their good side. They will reason that if you just wanted to improve your standing in their eyes, that you would compliment them to their face.[44]

If you have the chance to play the role of carrier pigeon, take it! Pass on all the compliments you can. Not only will you improve the relationship between the initiator and their intended target, but you'll also further your own reputation as a positive person who likes to make others happy. If everyone passed on "positive gossip," imagine how much more pleasant the world would be!

The Indirect (Or "Implied") Compliment

Rather than simply telling someone that you admire them for a specific reason, you can make a remark that implies that they possess certain qualities. Implied compliments work best in situations that call for a degree of problem solving. You can ask the target for help, and take the opportunity to admire their skills at the same time. For example, look at the following pair of compliments:

Direct compliment: "You're so smart."
Indirect compliment: "I don't get the points the author is making in this article, but you probably will. Could you help me make sense of it?"

Direct compliment: "You always look good. You have a real sense of style."
Indirect compliment: "I'm not sure what to wear for my sister's wedding. I need some expert help! Would you come shopping with me on Friday?"

Both examples make reference to a positive quality, but because these references are presented within a broader context, they are not as brash as a direct compliment.

---

[44] Lowndes, L. (1999). *How To Talk To Anyone*. Glasgow: Omnia Books Ltd.

Include A Question

Have you ever given someone a compliment, only to be met with an awkward silence? There's a simple trick that will ensure this never happens again. All you have to do is deliver the compliment, then follow it up immediately with a relevant question. "You are so good at drawing!" is a nice compliment. However, "You are so good at drawing, how did you learn?" is better, because it provides you with a bridge to other topics of conversation. It lets the other person talk about the time they went to art college, or the resources they use to teach themselves, or the hours it takes to create a piece of art, and so on. Ending a compliment with a question also signals to your target that you are not just trying to flatter them, but that you care about the broader context of their talents and abilities.

You should also remember that someone might be surprised to get a sincere compliment, and may not be able to respond for a few seconds. Even if you add a question on the end, they may need to gather their thoughts. Try not to take this personally.

How To Accept A Compliment

When someone gives you a compliment, always accept it graciously. We all know people who reject any compliment within a ten-mile radius. **I'm all for being humble, but resisting a sincere compliment is rude.** When someone praises you, they are essentially saying, "I have made this judgment, and I want to share my opinion." If you knock them back, you are implying that you doubt their ability to assess a situation and devise their own opinion.

The best response is a warm, "Thank you, that's really nice of you," accompanied by a smile.[45] Make them feel good for trying to make you feel good! **It doesn't matter whether or not you agree with their appraisal.** Think of a compliment as a gift. You'd never unwrap a gift and then throw it back in someone's face, would you? Even if you don't think a compliment is sincere, treat the giver as though they acted with the best of intentions.

---

[45] Whitmore, J. (2014). *How to Receive a Compliment Without Being Awkward About It.* entrepreneur.com

Chapter 13: How To Ask Excellent Questions

Why do we have conversations in the first place? Often, it's because we need to gain insight into a particular situation, or because we want to understand what someone else is thinking. Asking the right questions is a skill that will make all the difference in every area of your life. Being able to answer questions shows that you are educated and knowledgeable, but knowing how to ask them is the mark of good judgment and a willingness to learn.

Social Questions – Striking Up Rapport & Moving Beyond Small Talk

As you know, people who talk only about themselves are seen as rude and boring. Asking questions is the best way of switching the spotlight onto your conversation partner. A good question will encourage the other person to open up, thus creating a sense of rapport and intimacy between you. If you've ever overheard a conversation between two people that was based on thoughtful questions, you'll know that they can soon turn complete strangers into two individuals on the fast track to friendship. They can also help you deepen a relationship with someone you already know, but have yet to really understand or connect with on any meaningful level. So, once you're past the small talk stage, how can you use questions to get to know someone better and pave the way for exciting conversations?

Share something about yourself before asking a personal question: There are a few useful findings from the world of psychology that I draw on when helping my clients ask better questions. First up, we have the principle of social reciprocity. This basically means that when someone does something nice for us, we feel compelled to do something for them in return. Robert Cialdini, one of the most famous psychologists in the world, covers this nicely in his book, *The Psychology Of Persuasion.* [46] People who are willing to talk about personal experiences and opinions are usually perceived as more likeable than those who stick to impersonal or generic topics.[47] Finally, when we tell someone else about ourselves, we are more likely to feel kindly towards them.[48]

---

[46] Cialdini, R.B. (2007). *Influence: The Psychology Of Persuasion.* New York: HarperBusiness.
[47] Collins, N.L., & Miller, L.C. (1994). Self-Disclosure and Liking: A Meta-Analytic Review. *Psychological Bulletin, 116, 3,* 457-475.
[48] Ibid.

Before you ask any personal questions, start off by disclosing something interesting about your feelings or life experiences. This creates an atmosphere of trust, and also encourages your conversation partner to share something of their own. If someone tells you something personal about themselves or their life, respond in kind. If you aren't prepared to answer a question, don't ask it of someone else. Answering in advance will also put someone at ease. For example, "I'd love to travel the world one day. What's your biggest dream?" is better than, "What is your ultimate dream?" Show that you are willing to be vulnerable, and they are more likely to trust you.

Questions That Build Intimacy: Arthur Aron's Closeness-Generating Procedure

In 1997, a psychologist called Arthur Aron carried out a study that was to become a landmark in the social sciences. He put pairs of strangers together, and then gave them a set of questions printed on slips of paper. Half the pairs were given a set of personal questions, and the other half were given a set of small talk-style questions instead.[49] Strangers who asked one another the "closeness-generating" questions felt a greater sense of connection and comfort with their partners. The moral of the story? Whenever possible, ask deep questions that go beyond facts and figures. To give you an idea of the difference between these categories, here are some examples taken directly from Aron's paper:

"Small talk" questions:
How did you celebrate last Halloween?
Where are you from?
Where did you go to high school?

"Closeness-generating" questions:
Would you like to be famous? In what way?
What is the greatest accomplishment of your life?
What, if anything, is too serious to be joked about?

---

[49] Aron, A., Melinat, E., Aron, E.N., Vallone, R.D., & Bator, R.J. (1997). The Experimental Generation of Interpersonal Closeness: A Procedure and Some Preliminary Findings. *Personality and Psychology Bulletin, 23, 4*, 363-377.

You'll have noticed that the closeness-generating questions require "deep" answers, and are personal in nature. You will have to use your judgment when deciding when to move from small talk to heavy hitting questions. Wait until you are in a state of strong rapport with the other person, and then you can gradually move from relatively "tame" questions to the deeper topics. Always be prepared to move the conversation to more trivial subjects if they show any signs of discomfort.

Use the "Parroting" technique to encourage further disclosure: The parroting technique helps shy people open up. All you have to do is take the final two or three words of their answer, and turn them into a question. [50] It's an easy, unobtrusive prompt that can yield more satisfactory answers. Parroting is also less formal than asking a question in its entirety. It might take a couple of rounds, but I'd estimate my success rate with this technique is around ninety-five per cent. For example:

You: "Have you ever thought about what it would be like to be famous?"
Them: "Yes. I'm not sure I'd really like it. All those photographers."
You: "The photographers?"
Them: "The paparazzi would come after me!"
You: "Come after you?"
Them: "Yes. Did you see that story about the movie star who…"

Listen for clues: If you pay close attention to the innocent (or not so innocent) comments someone makes, you will notice that they will make reference to the same topic(s) on multiple occasions. This gives you a valuable starting point for meaningful questions that tap into their deepest passions. I'll show you how this can work in practice.

I recently met a new contact for a business lunch. As we sat down, she brushed a spot of dried mud from her skirt. "Oh, look at that!" she said, "That's my dog's fault. He's always jumping up at me when I try to leave the house." The conversation then turned to my contact's business, and their latest products. She talked about their range of remote webcams and

---

[50] Lowndes, L. (1999). *How To Talk To Anyone*. Glasgow: Omnia Books Ltd.

viewing apps. "Of course, they're great for parents who want to check on kids and babysitters," she said. "And dog owners like them too!" I started to get the message – this woman was crazy about dogs. **When someone is truly passionate about something, it usually pops up in conversation, even if the original topic is totally unrelated.**

The meeting was proceeding well, but it lacked that special spark that makes for a truly outstanding conversation. Over dessert, I casually mentioned that I was looking forward to visiting my sister soon. "It's always great to spend time on her farm," I said. "You know, to get away from it all. And she has these adorable dogs! You mentioned you had a dog...?" I didn't need to say much more. That was all the permission she needed. When the time came for us to part ways, she insisted that we meet up in the near future, and that I was "such good conversation." Of course, all I'd done was ask a simple but well-chosen question. This trick can build rapport in seconds.

Frame your question as something worthy of excitement: Before you even ask a question, take the opportunity to influence the way in which the other person will perceive it. If you say, "Now, here's a good question...," your listener is more likely to assume that whatever you ask is going to be interesting than if you say, "I know this is an obvious question, but...."

Ask meaningful "we" questions: If you can combine a "we" question with an issue that is important to your conversation partner, you're on to a winner. Note that both parts of the equation need to be in place. A trivial "we" question, such as, "Do you think we'll have to stay five extra minutes again at the end of this meeting?" is a nice piece of small talk, but isn't going to build a high level of rapport or encourage personal disclosure. However, questions like, "So, do you think we'll be bought out by the end of the year?" or "Do you think we should all give more money to charity?" invite someone to think of you as members of the same team, and disclose their personal opinions at the same time. This will boost rapport and lead to interesting discussions.

How To Ask Questions When You Need Factual Answers

Of course, some questions serve one purpose only – to elicit factual information. You'll use these in business settings, and when you need to hone in on objective facts as opposed to how someone is feeling. Before you ask the question, make sure you know what you want to achieve. For example, you might be looking to gain an in-depth understanding of how a department in your organization works, or you may be keen to learn precisely how a particular medical procedure is carried out. Keep your objective at the forefront of your mind, as this will guide you during the conversation.

Make Sure You're Asking The Right Person

The person with the most knowledge on a topic isn't always in the best position to answer your question. We all know people who have a great grasp of a subject, but are not very good at communicating information. Ideally, you need to ask someone who has relevant background knowledge, the ability to express themselves, and the confidence required to assert their opinions. Obviously, you won't always have access to someone who perfectly fits that description, but these three criteria can help you narrow down your options. This is particularly relevant if your question is technical, or requires input from someone with a high level of expertise.

If you are approaching someone you don't know in the hope that they will help you answer an important question, do a little background research first. Consider where this person is from, their level of education, their interests, and even (if the information is available) their personality type. Social media can be a great tool here! If you have a mutual friend, ask them for advice if possible. For example, you could ask, "I'm going to have a meeting with X, to ask them about Y. Any tips to help me have a productive conversation with them?"

Don't Waste Anyone's Time

Before asking a question, make sure that you've exhausted all the obvious avenues first. It only takes a few seconds to use Google, after all. Even when your own research doesn't turn up the answers you need, you should still be willing to show that you've made the effort. For example, "I've looked through the relevant chapter in the textbook and I've been doing some research online, but I just can't understand this topic. Can you explain it?" will get a more sympathetic response than, "I just don't get this. Can you explain it to me?"

My friend Jack is a computer science professor. He once told me that his weakest students are those who don't understand how to use their initiative. They tend to email him every time they hit a stumbling block, rather than making the effort to use the many online resources available to them. Jack doesn't mind helping his students out (he loves passing on his knowledge!), but fielding the same basic questions day after day really annoys him. He is much more likely to respond positively to a student who has made a genuine effort to help themselves before coming to him.

If you get the impression that someone thinks you have wasted their time, ask them what you could do to help yourself in the future. This gives them the chance to pass on links to books, websites and other resources that will allow you to come up with answers independently.

When it comes to actually formulating your question, bear in mind the following points:[51]

Start with the basics if you need clarification: If you aren't sure what a piece of jargon means, ask! It's better to risk mild embarrassment than it is to stay quiet and make a costly mistake later.

Ask only one question at a time: No one likes to be on the receiving end of a barrage of questions, and combining multiple questions into one long rambling sentence is a sure way of annoying or confusing someone. Establish the questions you need answering, and think of the most logical order in which to ask them. If possible, write them as a list on a piece of paper or as a note on your phone. This might seem a bit strange if you are talking to a friend or relative (as opposed to a boss or professor), but it's a useful tool that will keep you on track. If you are asking several important questions, it's a good idea to take notes or record the conversation for review at a later date.

---

[51] Snow, S. (2012). *The One Conversational Tool That Will Make You Better At Absolutely Everything*. fastcompany.com

If it's a complex question, let them know from the outset: Let the other person know if you need to ask them an especially difficult question. Give them the opportunity to clear their mind so that they focus their full attention on what you are about to say.

Know when to interrupt: Generally, it's rude to interrupt someone if they are speaking, and the rule still applies if you have just asked them a question. However, there are times when interrupting is the most sensible course of action. For example, if someone answers your question but then begins to venture far away from the topic at hand, a simple, "I'm sorry to interrupt, but I just want to clarify something" can work to get the conversation back on track. This trick also works if the other person didn't quite understand your question, and gave you an unexpected answer that doesn't make sense.

Don't get nervous if they pause for thought: If the other person stops talking for a moment, or waits several seconds before launching into their answer, don't take it as a sign that you asked the wrong sort of question. When someone pauses to gather their thoughts, they are paying you the compliment of treating your question as a matter worthy of serious consideration. Give them the space they need. Do not jump in and start talking just for the sake of filling the silence.

Do not lead someone down a particular path: If you want to know what someone really thinks, avoid asking them a leading question. Leading questions are those that encourage someone to answer in a particular way. For example, look at the following pairs of questions:

Leading question: "What problems are you facing on this project?"
Non-leading question: "Could you tell me how this project is going?"

Leading question: "Wouldn't it be a good idea to donate more money to this charity?"
Non-leading question: "What are your thoughts on the amount of money we currently donate to this charity?"

In the first example, the leading question assumes that the other person is facing some problems, which will encourage them to dwell on the negative aspects of their experience. The alternative allows for answers that focus on good news too, which would result in a more balanced assessment of the situation. In the second example, the leading question suggests that donating more money to the charity is obviously a good idea, thus encouraging the respondent to agree. The non-leading question is open-ended, allowing the other person the chance to voice their true opinions on the size of the donation.

Try another approach if the first doesn't work: We all have our own quirks and preferences when it comes to asking and answering questions. For example, some people dislike direct questions, and interpret them as a kind of conversational assault. Don't be discouraged if you hit a wall. Think of a different way of phrasing the question. Humor can also be a powerful tool in getting answers. A simple joke such as, "C'mon, the suspense is killing me here!" can lighten the mood, help your target relax, and therefore increase the likelihood that they will give you the answer you need.

Using Questions To Change Someone's Mind

Questions don't just work as a means of eliciting information. They can also be used to change someone's mind, or at least get them to consider alternative points of view. When trying to convince someone to change their mind, most people try to lay out a logical argument, or make a passionate plea as to why their view is right and the other person's opinion is wrong. But when you take a minute to think about it, you'll realize that this doesn't often work. As soon as someone works out that you are on a mission to change their mind, the metaphorical shutters go down.

You'll have better luck if you ask well-chosen, open-ended questions that let a person challenge their own assumptions. We tend to approve of an idea or suggestion if we thought of it first – or at least, if we *think* we thought of it first. Therefore, encouraging someone to question their own worldview will often yield better results than trying to railroad them into accepting your opinion as fact.

Asking a chain of well-chosen questions gets someone to look at their own views from another angle, which might trigger fresh insights. This is pretty much what the best therapists do. They don't tell their clients what to think. Instead, they use the fine art of asking questions to help the client come to their own conclusions. When a therapist wants to suggest that a client looks at their situation in a new light, they only do so once the latter has had the chance to air their thoughts.

You can use the following questions to establish what someone thinks about a certain issue:

"Could you tell me what you think about that?"

"How do you feel about this particular issue?"

"I'm really interested in your opinion. Would you mind telling me what you think?"

Once you have a good understanding of what they believe, you can encourage them to evaluate their beliefs using the following questions:

"How did you arrive at that conclusion?"

"When people argue with you on this issue, what points do they try to make?"

"Are there any facts your theory can't explain?"

"What evidence, if any, would change your mind?"

"Do you have any friends who hold opposing beliefs?"

Listening carefully to their answers without interjecting will make them feel as though you are truly interested in what they have to say. In turn, they will be more likely to entertain your own views as well as evaluating their own opinions. Only once they are in a receptive state of mind should you then put forward your own perspective on the matter. Obviously, there is no guarantee that they will take your views on board, but at the very least, you'll have enjoyed a respectful exchange of opinions.

Asking For A Favor – "Can" Versus "Will"

What about asking someone to grant you a favor? Appeal to someone's sense of pride, and your chances of success increase. All you have to do is substitute "can" for "would" or "will."

"Would you please help me find the conference center?" is less effective than, "Can you please help me find the conference center?" When you ask someone whether they *can* do something, they immediately start to take assess their own capabilities. Internally, they will arrive at either a "Yes," a "No," or a "Maybe." Their answer is more likely to reflect their capabilities, not their desire to help you. "Can I or can't I?" is easier to answer than, "Will I help this person or not?"

Asking the right questions is a key conversation skill. The next time you succeed in getting a helpful answer out of someone, reflect on how you asked your question, and file that strategy away for future use. Remember that what works with one person may not work so well with another, so be prepared to tailor you approach as necessary.

Chapter 14: How To Handle Heated Discussions

Arguments and heated discussions are inevitable. Unless you take a completely passive approach in every area of your life (which I wouldn't recommend!), you will have to navigate tough discussions from time to time. Luckily, there are a few easy tricks you can use that will make all the difference between a peaceful resolution and an ugly scene.

Stop fearing anger as an emotion: Anger, whether in yourself or someone else, is not intrinsically bad. Anger is a normal human emotion. In fact, it's healthy to get angry from time to time, because it forces us to recognize when something needs to change. **The problem isn't the feeling, but how it's expressed.** When you find yourself getting angry, give yourself permission to feel mad. Remind yourself that all feelings are temporary, and you won't be angry forever. If you are on the receiving end of someone else's anger, remember that their fury is bound to fade at some point. **Shift your focus to conflict resolution, rather than worrying about how to overcome your underlying feelings.**

Let the other party know exactly what you want: If someone suspects that you have an ulterior motive, or isn't sure what you are trying to achieve, they are liable to become defensive. This promotes an atmosphere of tension. As soon as possible, state what you want to achieve, and tell the other person that you hope the two of you can work together in coming up with a mutually satisfying outcome. **Make it clear that you aren't looking to fight for the sake of it, but rather that you are attempting to solve a problem.** Don't aim to "win" an argument or prove your point. Try to build a positive relationship instead.[52] Never resort to personal insults or snide remarks.

Whatever you say, say it at your usual volume: It's normal to raise your voice when you're mad, right? Yes, but it's not helpful. Yelling or screaming might intimidate someone, but it will not win their respect, and it definitely isn't going to help you hold a constructive conversation. Think of conflict as a cycle. If you speak in a loud tone of voice, this signals to the other person that you are physically aroused and ready for a fight. Their nervous system will automatically kick in, and they will also get ready for combat. This happens on an automatic

---

[52] Carrier Management. (2017). *How to Keep Your Conversations on Track and Productive.* carriermanagement.com

level, and the process takes just a couple of seconds. The more aggressive you appear – and you will indeed appear aggressive if you talk loudly, or use confrontational body language – the more fired up the other person will become. This effect can result in two people screaming at one another. You can prevent this from happening by keeping your voice steady. Do not fall into the trap of trying to yell over someone else in an attempt to make yourself heard. A better tactic is to remain silent until they have finished speaking (or shouting). Tell them, "If you talk over me, I'm going to stop engaging with you, because it's pointless for us to both talk at the same time."

Know when to keep quiet: What's the best thing to say when someone is so angry that they start ranting at you? Absolutely nothing. **Give them a few minutes to get their rage out of their system.** No matter what they say, or what you think of their opinions, bite your tongue. Trying to interrupt someone who is on a verbal rampage is like trying to stop a rhino from charging. It's pointless, and you may get seriously hurt. Someone in this state is beyond reason. They just want to vent their feelings, and reassure themselves that someone is listening to their point of view. Eventually, they will run out of energy and slow down. If you remain silent, they will realize that they are the only one speaking, and that to an onlooker, they appear rather ridiculous.

Stick to the issue at hand: Never assume that another person has good communication skills. Be prepared to come up against weak arguments and dirty tactics. For example, people with poor conflict resolution skills tend to drag up the past when they fight. This is known as "stockpiling."[53] If you've ever been arguing with someone who suddenly raises a long-forgotten conflict you thought had been resolved weeks, months, or even years ago, you'll know how disorienting this move can be!

I remember witnessing a great example of stockpiling back when I worked as a middle manager in a large HR department. I was in a meeting with several other members of the team, ranging from junior employees to the head of HR. The topic of conversation was the company's intern recruitment process. Approximately one-half of those at the table thought that the

---

[53] Goldsmith, B. (2009). *Top 10 Tools to Avoid Ugly Arguments*. psychologytoday.com

existing protocol was just fine. The other half (myself included) thought that it warranted a thorough evaluation, because it had remained unchanged for three years. An argument broke out between two team members. As they slung points back and forth, it became harder to keep up with what they were actually saying.

However, we all heard one party when they yelled, "And you messed up when it came to organizing the Christmas party last year! You can't even plan a work social!" My boss then had to step in. It might seem ludicrous, but this kind of stockpiling is pretty common. When someone wants to make a point, or just hurt someone else, they will rack their brains for something to throw at their target. Don't take it personally, and don't get drawn in. Stockpiling can also be a diversionary tactic – if you are getting close to the truth, or making a strong argument, someone who is annoyed at you might attempt to throw you off-track by bringing up random topics.

Ignore irrelevant points. Repeat the last thing you said before the other person went off on a tangent. You might have to do this several times to get your message across, i.e. that you are only willing to talk about the problems affecting you both in the here and now. Keep restating what you need to know until they either provide you with the information you need, or the situation escalates to a point at which it turns out that they are beyond reason. If they are literally incapable of an adult discussion, you can at least walk away knowing that you did your best. If you absolutely must work with this person to solve a serious problem, reschedule your discussion for another day.

When dealing with a really difficult person, asking a third party for help might be the best option. For example, if you can't seem to have a constructive conversation with a colleague about a situation at work, ask a co-worker or supervisor to act as mediator, or at least request that they sit in on the next discussion and take notes. Sometimes, just knowing that another party is watching the argument unfold is enough to make someone think twice before acting in an aggressive or unhelpful manner.

Don't make ultimatums: An ultimatum is a threat. What do people do when they encounter a threat? They go into fight or flight mode, of course! That's not what you want to happen when emotions are running high.[54] Stark demands such as, "You either need to agree, or be prepared to lose your job!" or "If you don't start making more time for me in the evenings, this relationship is finished!" don't help. Ultimatums are especially liable to backfire when the other person has a short temper or a rebellious streak, because they will get mad at you for even daring to issue them with an ultimatum in the first place.

Do not try to feign indifference: Acting as though you aren't too bothered by the issue at hand is another quick way to make someone angry and upset. They will feel as though they have two problems to solve: The original issue that prompted the discussion in the first place, and your apparent indifference. Listen to what the other person is saying, even if you think it's utter garbage.

If someone is goading you, call a halt to the conversation: Should you ever find yourself in an argument or discussion with someone who is just provoking you for the sake of it, it's time to call a time out. Once someone is in what I call, "Goad Mode," they lose the capacity for a rational exchange of views. Take ten minutes apart to cool off.

Do not tolerate verbal abuse: Anger is fine, and a heated exchange is sometimes exactly what is needed to clear the air. However, under no circumstances should you be expected to put up with verbal abuse. If someone is acting in an aggressive manner or using abusive language, remove yourself from the situation. There is no point trying to reason with someone who is content to fall back on abuse as a substitute for constructive dialogue. You also have to bear in mind that verbal abuse may escalate to physical violence, so walking away may be an important safety measure. If you absolutely must have a difficult conversation with someone who is prone to aggression, make sure you are not alone in the same room. Alternatively, conduct the conversation via phone or webcam, and keep a recording (check that this is legal in your state or country first).

---

[54] Ibid.

How To Handle A Heated Meeting

If you are in a management position, you may sometimes need to play the role of mediator during meetings. When a group of people gather to talk about sensitive matters, there is a strong likelihood that a heated exchange will result. It's a good idea to think in advance of each meeting whether controversial matters may arise, and what you will do about them. Here are a few strategies that will help you run a meeting in which tensions are likely to run high:

Establish your authority early on: Make sure that you are the first to arrive. Welcome everyone as they come in. This signals that you are taking the meeting seriously, and that you will be paying close attention to what everyone is saying. Ensure that you have as much background information as possible, both on the topic at hand and the people who will be in attendance. Your confidence will show through in your demeanor, and others will be more receptive to what you have to say.

As far as possible, structure the meeting in such a way that everyone will have the chance to voice their opinions on key issues. When people feel as though they are not being heard, or believe that they have been "shut out" of the discussion, they are liable to become angry and frustrated. Make it clear from the outset that everyone will have the chance to share their perspective. Once you establish a reputation as a manager who runs meetings in an efficient manner, people who may otherwise take the opportunity to push their opinions in an overly aggressive way will think twice before doing so.

Shut down crosstalk quickly: The moment two people begin speaking over one another, hold up one hand and say, "Stop there please. X is talking. When they have finished, you will have the chance to put your own view forward." As long as you are consistent in applying this rule, most people will respect it.[55]

Use "we" language to unite the group: When two or more people start to argue, identify the central issue that divides them and reframe it so that it becomes the group's problem instead.

---

[55] Eaton, S. (2011). *21 Leadership Tips for Chairing Difficult Meetings.* drsaraheaton.wordpress.com

This promotes a collaborative approach. For example, if two people are arguing about which type of accounting software is the best choice for the company, you could take the specific point of contention (i.e. "X is better than Y!") and tell the group, "OK, we have to consider which software we are going to use for keeping track of our accounts. Let's brainstorm this as a group." This takes the focus away from the argument between two people, and instead turns the problem into an issue for everyone to tackle together.

Slow down and summarize: If two or more people are putting forward ideas at a rapid rate, halt the meeting and tell those present that you are going to summarize the ideas expressed as you understand them. For example, you might say, "Adam, as far as I understand, you are proposing that we use this set of figures." You would then give Adam the opportunity to correct you if necessary. You would then summarize the view of anyone opposing him. This allows each party to feel as though their views are being heard, and it also ensures that everyone present understands each person's perspective.[56]

Use questions to handle diversions and shut down hostility: Questions such as, "I'm not sure I understand - how does your argument help us find a solution to the problem?," "Are you saying that we need to move in a particular direction here?," and "Can you summarize your conclusions for us?" can be an efficient means of encouraging someone to get back on track.

How To Handle An Insult

No one enjoys being on the receiving end of an insult, but once you know how to handle them, you'll be prepared for even the rudest of remarks.

See the insult as an opportunity to impress anyone who happens to be watching: If someone insults you whilst other people are watching, everyone in the group will watch to see how you respond. If you handle the situation in a calm, dignified manner, they will respect you more as a result.

---

[56] MindTools. (2017). *Managing Conflicts in Meetings.* mindtools.com

Make a decision on whether to call them out: Most insults are given with the intention of getting some kind of reaction from the victim. However, whether or not you should call the other person out depends on the situation. Steve Dinkin, president of the National Conflict Resolution Center, says that mild or occasional insults – known as "micro-insults" - are best ignored.[57] If you can stay calm and avoid engaging with the person who has insulted you, they will receive no return on their investment. This means that you can "win" without actually having to do anything.

Remember that someone might just be having a bad day, or they may have failed to recognize how their remark sounded to others. They may not have intended to insult you at all. Who hasn't said something that was intended as a neutral remark, or even a compliment, only to accidentally cause offence? If there is any chance that the person who offended you might not have intended their comment as an insult, assume the best (i.e., that they just worded their thoughts in a clumsy way) and let it go.

On the other hand, if someone has just made an aggressive or vulgar remark to your face, or they repeatedly throw out micro-insults, you need to react. Otherwise, you risk appearing weak in front of others. In these situations, a passive response will invite further abuse. I want to be absolutely clear – no one deserves to be mistreated. However, the way you respond makes a big difference to how an individual will treat you in the future.

There isn't a single, universal "trick" for calling someone out. The best tactic will depend on the situation, the number of other people present, the nature of the insult, and your personality. **Here are a couple of tips:**

1. *Ask a question:* Etiquette expert Diane Gottsman, who specializes in business communication training, has some excellent advice on how to deal with a rude remark – respond with a question.[58] This strategy allows you to call them out on their behavior without resorting to aggressive or inflammatory remarks of your own.

---

[57] Malugani, M. (2017). *Seven Tips for Dealing with Office Insults.* monster.com
[58] Gottsman, D. (2013). *Business Etiquette: How to Handle an Offensive Remark.* huffingtonpost.com

The question you ask depends on the context. Sometimes, merely asking someone to clarify what they said can be enough to shame them into shutting up. For example, suppose you heard a colleague mutter, "You're so incompetent." You could ask loudly, "Sorry, I didn't hear you. I think you just said I am incompetent, is that right?" Another approach is to simply ask, "Why do you think that?" If they give a nonsensical response, ask them the same question again. They will soon realize how stupid they look in front of others, which should be enough to deter them from insulting you in the future.

2. *State your feelings and next steps:* An alternative approach is to state how you feel about the comment, why it is unhelpful, and what you will do if they do not stop. For example, you might say, "I don't like it when you insult me like that. It isn't going to help our team solve this problem. If you keep insulting me, I'm going to leave the room."[59] This is a calm, dignified way of handling the situation which may work well if you dislike confrontation and feel too intimidated to ask them a question.

   This tactic also allows you to highlight the fact that they are behaving unprofessionally. If you remind someone that they are acting in a manner wholly unsuitable to the situation, this is often enough to shut them down. For example, if someone insults you during a meeting, you might say, "I don't think engaging in petty insults is very professional. Let's focus on actually sorting out the problems on the agenda."

3. *Tackle them directly – but do so in private:* If you have been insulted by a particular person more than once, and calling them out in the moment hasn't worked, set up a one-on-one conversation (but in a public place, such as a café, so that you can leave quickly if the situation escalates). In a neutral tone of voice, tell them how their behavior has made you feel. Tell them that if they continue to act in this manner, you will take the matter to a person in authority or enact other appropriate measures such as issuing them with a written warning (if you are in a position of authority). Stating your boundaries lets the other person know that you are not going to tolerate their behavior.

---

59 QuickBase. (2012). *How to Respond When You're Verbally Attacked at Work.* quickbase.com

4. *Don't sling an insult in return:* By responding with an offensive remark of your own, you are lowering yourself to the level of the other person, and increasing the likelihood of an all-out argument.

5. *Use humor with care:* If you have a quick wit, your first instinct might be to fire off a sharp retort. However, making fun of the person who is making fun of you sets the stage for needless conflict. If others are watching, you may be surprised to find that they begin to side with the original perpetrator rather than you, especially if you are great at coming up with really cutting remarks.[60]

Insults are seldom a reflection of your character or flaws. As cliché as this may sound, they say more about the other person. Often, an insult is an attempt to grab power, or bolster a fragile sense of self. As a rule, don't take them personally. If someone insults you, think of them as a schoolyard bully who is attempting to make themselves feel better and bolster their status in the eyes of the other kids watching. Pretty pathetic, isn't it? Remember, even if someone else is acting like a child, you can always make the decision to act like a responsible adult.

How To Apologize

No one is right all the time. On occasion, you need to apologize to someone, and admit that you made a mistake in how you handled an issue or conversation. If you are wondering how best to make an apology, you are ahead of the game. Most people are reluctant to admit that they could possibly have screwed up in the first place! Give yourself some credit for your good manners and emotional intelligence. The best and most well-respected communicators understand the value of a sincere apology. Here's how to give an apology that will smooth over a difficult situation:

Show that you understand how the other person feels: Most of the time, someone who wants an apology is primarily looking for evidence that someone cares about their feelings. Use their own words if possible, in order to minimize the chance of further misunderstandings. For

---

[60] Gottsman, D. (2013). *Business Etiquette: How to Handle an Offensive Remark.* huffingtonpost.com

example, if someone told you during a fight that they were "really hurt" by what you said, use these exact words when you apologize. "I know I caused you to feel really hurt by what I said, and I apologize for saying those things," would be a good way of phrasing your apology. If they correct you, don't argue – they know better than you how they felt at the time!

Give an explanation, not an excuse: No one likes to hear excuses. Even a believable excuse is no substitute for a straightforward acknowledgement of your actions. By all means tell someone why you acted as you did, but always emphasize that you could have chosen to behave in a different way. Look at the example below:

Excuse-based apology: "Sorry, I know I said I'd call, but I was busy."

Explanation-based apology: "Sorry, I know I said I'd call. Things got very busy at work and I had to stay late. However, I knew I should have sent you a text or email instead, and I'm sorry that I didn't get in touch to let you know what was happening."

The explanation-based apology is more thoughtful, and gives the recipient a chance to think about the situation in a broader context. Rather than seeing the other person as a thoughtless individual who doesn't care enough about their feelings to make a quick phone call, they are more likely to see them as a person who meant to get in touch, but was under a lot of pressure at work. Careful explanation-based apologies can open the door to better mutual understanding, which in turn can enhance a relationship. To continue with the example above, the recipient of the apology might feel compelled to ask, "You seem very busy lately – what exactly is the problem at work?"

Tell them what you are doing to make amends, and what preventative measures you plan to take: An apology isn't much good if the same situation is likely to occur again. You need to let the injured party know what you are going to do to prevent it happening in the future. For example, if your dog escapes from your yard and digs up your neighbor's lawn, it's not enough to merely apologize for the damage. You should offer to pay for a gardener to fix it, and then tell your neighbor what you are going to do to prevent your dog escaping again.

Don't demand that the other person accept your apology: Social convention and good manners dictate that we accept an apology, but you should never expect someone to say, "Thank you so much! I fully accept your apology, and now harbor no negative feelings towards you!" Life is rarely so simple. The other person might want to clarify the issue by asking you some questions, or they might want to emphasize again how hurt they feel. Employ your best listening skills, and show that you are looking to understand how to avoid hurting them again in the future.

Once you have apologized, it's time to move on from the situation. If the conflict is resolved and the other person accepts your apology, great! If they don't, you need to accept that they might need some time to process what has happened. Also, bear in mind that the other person might feel as though they are allowing you off the hook by accepting your apology. This is an emotionally immature approach, but some people know no better. Try not to take it personally. As long as you've played your role in repairing the relationship, all you can do is let it go.

Chapter 15: How To Persuade Someone Of Your Opinion

Have you ever found yourself in a situation where you needed to influence someone else? Changing someone's attitude isn't easy if you are unprepared. Luckily, persuasion is a well-researched area of psychology, and the field has yielded lots of useful findings. In this chapter, I'm going to share the magic ingredients that will supercharge your powers of persuasion.

When you were in school or college, your teachers probably taught you how to write a persuasive paper. That's all well and good, but it isn't adequate preparation for making a convincing argument face-to-face. When you are dealing with a human being, logic and reason isn't enough. You also need to be aware how to tap into their emotions, and take advantage of the factors people take into account when deciding whether they find a message convincing. I'd argue that before you even think about how you plan to present your points in a logical manner, you need to understand how the average person processes information.

The father of persuasion research, Robert Cialdini, has identified several key factors that go some way in determining the success of an argument. These include authority, likeability, reciprocity, and consensus.[61] Let's take these factors one by one, and look at how they can help you change someone's mind, or get them to follow a particular course of action. Later in the chapter, I'll give you a few hints on how to lay out your case in a logical manner.

Authority: Make It Clear Why You Are Qualified To Talk About The Issue

It's no secret that companies put testimonies by "experts" and Ph.Ds. on their products to improve sales. Put simply, when people see that an expert has (supposedly) approved of the product, they are likely to think that it must, by definition, be good. The same principle applies in the context of a debate. If someone in authority says something, people tend to assume that it must be true, particularly if they are a renowned expert on the topic. This cognitive bias probably occurs because from an early age, we are taught that people with experience in a particular field, or those holding a special title, are naturally qualified to speak on a subject.

---

[61] Kenrick, D.T. (2012). *The 6 Principles of Persuasion.* psychologytoday.com

Therefore, we find their arguments more persuasive.[62]

If there's a good reason why you're qualified to put forth your opinion, emphasize it! To use a simple example, if you are trying to convince someone that artificial sweeteners are not harmful to health, and you have a degree in the biological or chemical sciences, mentioning this fact adds to your credibility. Note that it doesn't really matter whether your qualification is actually relevant – it just has to *appear* relevant.

If you don't happen to have an academic or vocational qualification, don't worry – there are other ways to add to your credibility. The easiest way is to hijack someone else's authority by quoting or paraphrasing them. To continue with the example above, you might say, "I've looked into this issue. I can tell you that Dr. X, an expert in this field, says that artificial sweeteners pose no threat to health." Offer to send the other person links to books and articles. Most people won't bother taking you up on it, but the fact that you are willing to send primary sources will send the impression that you have a lot of confidence in your argument.

You can also establish credibility by communicating that you have taken the time to gain an in-depth knowledge on both the issue at hand, and on subjects that are tangentially related.[63] For example, if you are arguing that marijuana causes cancer, being able to speak confidently on cancer as a general topic will boost your authority. You will appear to have considered the issue at length if you seem to know a lot about the background issues, not just a specific point of debate.

Likeability: Do You Come Across As A Likeable Person?

Likeable people are at an advantage when it comes to putting forward an argument. Because our experience of the world teaches us that individuals usually agree with their friends, we tend to adopt the rule, "If I like someone, I probably agree with them."[64] Therefore, it's smart

[62] Tormala, Z.L., Brinol, P., & Petty, R.E. (2006). When credibility attacks: The reverse impact of source credibility on persuasion. *Journal of Experimental Social Psychology, 42,* 684-691.
[63] Heath, C., & Heath, D. (2008). *Made to Stick: Why Some Ideas Take Hold & Others Come Unstuck.* Sevenoaks: Cornerstone Digital.
[64] Chaiken, S. (1980). Heuristic Versus Systematic Information Processing and the Use of Source Versus Message Cues in Persuasion. *Journal of Personality and Social Psychology, 39, 5,* 752-766.

to tap into this unconscious "rule of thumb" by making yourself likeable. By following the conversation skills in this book, you'll be off to a great start. Showing empathy, building rapport, and showing a genuine interest in what another person has to say will make you more appealing. Compliments can also make you appear more likeable, but be careful not to overdo them, or the other person will feel as though they are on the receiving end of manipulation.

Psychologists have established that, in general, physically attractive sources are more persuasive than unattractive people.[65] However, this rule doesn't hold under all conditions. When people are heavily invested in an argument, they are willing to pay more attention to the finer details of the points someone is making, rather than their appearance.[66] Still, it doesn't hurt to make sure that you are looking good when putting forward your opinion!

Reciprocity: Does The Other Person Feel As Though They "Owe" You?

According to the role of social reciprocity, when someone does something "nice" for us, we tend to assume that we owe them a favor in return. Most of the time, this principle plays out over trivial matters. For example, if you agree to look after your neighbor's dog whilst they are on vacation, they will probably agree to water your houseplants when you go on a two-week business trip.

However, this also applies in debates and discussions. If you appear to take someone's advice on board, or agree to one of their suggestions, you leave them feeling indebted to you. When you then ask them to agree with you, or to go along with one of your own ideas – which is what you are trying to do when making an argument – they are more likely to fall in line.[67] The trick is to pick your battles. Sometimes, going along with what someone wants for the sake of lowering their resistance to your own ideas is worth the payoff.

For example, if you want to persuade your colleague to work from home on Thursdays instead of Wednesdays because it would be more convenient for your own schedule, your

[65] DeBono, K.G., & Harnish, R.J. (1988). Source Expertise, Source Attractiveness, and the Processing of Persuasive Information: A Functional Approach. *Journal of Personality and Social Psychology, 55, 4,* 541-546.
[66] Ibid.
[67] Rieck, D. (1997). *Influence and Persuasion: The Rule of Reciprocity.* directcreative.com

chances of success will be higher if you agree to one of their own requests in advance. Giving a "free gift" also works well. This doesn't have to be a physical item. For example, it can take the form of an offer to help on a project. For maximum effect, allow a few hours (or even days) to elapse between offering a gift/help and trying to persuade someone to change their attitudes or behavior.

Consensus: Can You Apply The Principle Of Social Proof?

Humans tend to fall back on a set of default rules when making decisions. Psychologists refer to these as "heuristics." One common heuristic goes like this: "If lots of people like something, it's probably good." Another similar "rule" most of us follow is, "If lots of people believe that something is true, it probably is." These rules save us time and effort. This heuristic is also known as, "The Rule of Social Proof."

You can take advantage of this heuristic by telling someone that lots of other people have already adopted a particular opinion, or that their lives have improved as a result of adopting this view. This will trigger the other person's natural desire to conform to what everyone else is doing.[68] For example, you could:

Tell the other person that X% of the population hold a particular opinion;
Tell the other person that most of their friends and colleagues have already been convinced of your opinion;
Tell the other person that you know someone else who adopted the very same opinion or approach that you are putting forward, and that they had great results.

Of course, this will not work on everyone. Some people make a point of evaluating an argument point by point. However, you'll find that most folk are swayed by social proof.

---

[68] Ibid.

How To Lay Out Your Argument

Now that you have an appreciation of the factors that make persuasion more or less likely, it's time to plan how you will present your points! Follow these steps:

1. *State why the issue is important:* No one will bother listening to an argument that seems utterly irrelevant to their lives. Open with a statement or idea that will grab your listener's attention. For example, "If we don't address climate change, your food supply will be at risk!" is a captivating opener.

2. *Summarize your stance:* Let people know where you stand, and do so early. Don't leave them wondering about your motives. For example, "I'm absolutely against this new hiring policy, and I want to see it changed," is a definitive statement that prepares your listener for the points you are about to make.

3. *Establish your credibility:* Tell them why you are qualified to talk about the subject. For example, "As someone with five years of experience in accountancy, I'd argue..." establishes you as a trustworthy source.

4. *Use specific statistics:* Once you have laid the groundwork, you can start drawing on reliable sources. Make sure you are familiar with the numbers in advance, and be able to summarize them within a few seconds.

5. *Draw on case studies:* After establishing that your argument has some empirical backing, you should then use a case study or story to back up your point. Stories engage the listener's emotions, and show how statistics (which can be a bit dull on their own) translate into everyday life. Add a sentence underlining why the issue is so significant.

   How might this work in practice? Let's say you are making a case to your HR manager. Their harassment policies are in dire need of an overhaul, and you want to persuade them to review their procedures. You might say, "I read on Business Insider that thirty per cent of college graduates feel bullied at work. Think back to last year – we had six reported cases of harassment. One member of the Finance team had to take five weeks of leave from work. She lost her job, and is pursuing legal action against us. Harassment is a problem we can't ignore if we want our workforce morale to improve."

6. *Acknowledge the listener's counterarguments:* For a variety of reasons, such as personal biases or resistance to change, your listener might be reluctant to take your points on board. They might come back with some counterarguments. Under no circumstances should you make them feel angry or disrespected by talking over them, or ignoring what they have to say. **Leave no point unaddressed.** If you can't provide a satisfactory answer, tell them that you will get back to them later. Never lie, because they might check up on your story later, and your credibility will be undermined if they discover that you tried to deceive them.

Demonstrating that you understand why people might be reluctant to accept your opinion or recommendation suggests to your listener that you have thought about the issue in depth. If you are feeling sufficiently confident, you can even pre-empt your listener's objections and respond to them before they come up in conversation. For example, "I know that you might think X, so I'd like to reassure you that Y" can work well in lowering your listener's defenses and making them more receptive to your ideas.

Tap Into Their Principles

If you can identify the other person's personal triggers, you can tailor your argument with their specific psychology in mind.[69] Note that everyone holds slightly different principles, and processes their emotions in a unique way. For example, let's suppose that you notice that a couple of your colleagues have taken vacations at short notice, leaving the rest of the team scrambling to get the work done at the last minute. As a result, you want to convince your manager that everyone in the department should be obliged to give at least four weeks' notice if they want to take more than five consecutive days of vacation. If your manager has a reputation as someone who values equality and a level playing field for all, you could explain

---

[69] Weller, C. (2014). *The Psychology Of Arguing: How To Outsmart Your Opponent (And Win) With Brain Power Alone.* medicaldaily.com

that if such a system were implemented, everyone in the workplace would be able to plan their work in good time – it would ensure that everyone in the department would receive equal treatment. This trigger word would tap into their personal priorities.

Bonus Tip: The Role Of Eye Contact

Has anyone ever told you, "Look me in the eye when I talk to you!" How did it make you feel? Intimidated, perhaps? It's true that a hard stare can inspire fear and compliance. However, dominant body language doesn't necessarily help someone win an argument. Aggressive eye contact certainly won't help your case. Julia Minson, a social psychologist based at Harvard, has demonstrated that when people are forced to look a speaker in the eye as the speaker makes their case, they are more likely to cling to their old opinions compared to participants who are told to focus on the speaker's mouth.[70] If you really want to convince someone (not just intimidate them into submission), it's better to build rapport by mirroring their body language instead. Aim for assertiveness, not dominance. Otherwise, the other person's defense mechanisms will kick in, and they won't be willing to truly listen to whatever you have to say.

---

[70] Chen, F.S., Minson, J.A., Schone, M., & Heinrichs, M. (2013). In the Eye of the Beholder. *Psychological Science, 24, 11,* 2254-2261.

Chapter 16: How To Make A Complaint With Grace

Graham is one of my favorite clients. He's a quiet, unassuming man with a gentle sense of humor. During our first training session, I asked how his week had gone. "Oh, it's gone pretty well, I guess," he said. I had the feeling that he was holding something back.

After a few seconds, he grimaced slightly. "OK, so it's not been that good! Yesterday, I had to return a suit to a store, because it had a rip in the sleeve. I really hate making complaints. I feel like I'm being a jerk." Does this sound familiar? Graham certainly isn't my only client who feels a sense of dread at the thought of telling someone, "This isn't acceptable."

I have also worked with people who have no problem with the idea of making their dissatisfaction known, but find that their complaints never get the results they need. It seems that lots of us could do with a few lessons in making gracious complaints that culminate in a happy resolution. So how can you get what you want, without coming across as a jerk?

Practice stating your grievance aloud: When you make a complaint, you are by default making a negative statement. Whilst some of us feel perfectly entitled to ask for whatever we want, most of us would rather avoid confrontation. If you feel nervous, your adrenal glands will kick in, and the adrenalin will make you feel even worse. Give yourself the best possible chance of remaining cool and collected. Practicing what you are going to say, whether it's on the phone or in person, can help you deliver your complaint in a calm manner.

Read up on your rights: Don't risk embarrassing yourself and wasting your own time by asking for something you aren't actually entitled to get. The Government has put together a website (ftc.gov) that outlines your rights as a consumer. When you know precisely what you are entitled to get, it becomes harder for someone to brush you off.[71] If you are making a complaint in the workplace, read your organization's policies beforehand.

Complain about a product or service, not a person: Getting personal might grab someone's

---

[71] Citizens Information. (2017). *How to make a consumer complaint*. citizensinformation.ie

attention, but it rarely does you any good in the end. No one likes to feel insulted, so referring to an employee as "incompetent," "foolish," or something worse will only aggravate the situation. If you are disappointed with the company then say so, but why take your aggression out on a customer service representative?

Most of the time, the person who sold you an item or set up your service isn't even the same person who will be on the receiving end of your complaint, so getting personal will often make you look plain stupid.

I was once standing in line to pay at my local hardware store. When the woman in front of me stepped up to the counter, she reached into her pocket before slamming down a packet of clothes pegs onto the counter. "I came in here last week. You told me these would be great for hanging out linen!" she spat. "But they've creased my shirts something awful. What have you got to say about that?" The clerk took a deep breath and said, "I'm sorry, Madam. I can give you a refund if you like. I think there must have been a miscommunication somewhere down the line, because I only started working here yesterday." I could hear the guy behind me attempt to suppress a chuckle.

Do not say things like, "I demand that whoever served me be fired immediately!" This type of statement just makes you look self-important and ignorant – only the company (and possibly, enforcing bodies) can make those sorts of decisions.

Don't be afraid to take it higher: If a customer service assistant or clerk can't help you with your complaint, ask to speak with their manager. This request might put some employees on the defensive, so make it clear that you are not questioning their competence (even if you are), you just want to resolve the issue with someone in a position of authority. If you are making a complaint over the phone, ask to "escalate" the call.[72]

Use objective language, rather than value judgments: Value-laden words that denote subjective judgment are more inflammatory than objective terms. For instance, telling an

---

[72] Mele, C. (2017). *How To Get Better Customer Service, and Skip the Rage.* nytimes.com

employee that you hate their "stupid" products or "hopeless" customer helpline is not going to do you any favors. You will get much better results if you use phrases such as:

"It looks to me as though this product is broken because..."
"When I called the helpline on (insert date here), they told me that..."
"If you look at the lining of this sleeve, you can see a one-inch tear..."

Use closed questions if you want or need to have the issue resolved and wrap up the conversation quickly: Closed questions are great if you want to learn exactly what a company is prepared to do. For instance, "Are you going to give me a refund on this product?" cuts straight to the heart of the matter, and can save you time. Of course, if you want to hear the reasoning behind a decision, open-ended questions are better. For example, if you have been refused a refund, you could ask, "Could you please explain your refunds policy to me, because I don't understand how you arrived at this decision?"

Use the broken record technique with stubborn or incompetent employees: Not only are many consumers bad at making complaints, but a lot of customer service staff are poor at offering customer service! Employees who don't care about their work have little incentive to actually help you, and their primary objective will be to get you out of their hair as soon as possible. Some will try and fob you off with phrases such as, "Sorry, there's nothing I can do," or "No, we can't help you once the warranty has expired."

When you come up against these individuals, you need to make it clear that ignoring you isn't in their best interests, because you are going to stick around until you get what you want. The moment they realize that trying to dissuade you from pursuing your complaint isn't going to work, they'll be forced to engage with you. The best way of triggering this attitude shift is to use the broken record technique. Simply state what you would like to happen in a calm, clear voice, and repeat it until the other person complies with your request.[73] The following are common phrases you may have to repeat several times:

[73] Changing Minds. (2017). *Broken Record.* changingminds.org

"Yes, I understand, but the product is faulty. I want a refund."

"Yes, I see your point, but I need to speak to the manager."

"Yes, I see where you are coming from, but this is still covered under the warranty."

"Yes, I see your point, but you have overcharged me."

Note that each of these phrases contains a polite acknowledgement, which implies that you respect the other person. This helps prevent the situation from escalating into conflict. At no point should you raise your voice, use intimidating body language, or allow yourself to be diverted from your primary objective. If someone really can't give you what you want, the broken record technique will still work – in most circumstances, they will at least feel obliged to grant you some kind of explanation for their poor service.

If you are complaining to a company, remind them that their reputation matters: The best form of advertising is still word of mouth, and a company lives or dies by its reputation. Tell the employee you are talking to that you won't be recommending their products or services to your friends and family, because you feel let down. This is more likely to work on senior managers, as they are typically more emotionally invested in the company. If you can talk to the director or owner directly, raising the issue of reputation is especially effective.

If you happen to have a significant following on social media, or are a respected authority in your field, you could politely remind them that their reputation could be damaged if you were to tell your followers or subscribers about their poor customer service. Letting a manager or director know that you could choose to exert your influence can be enough to sway them in the right direction. Don't threaten anyone, but if you have this kind of power, keep it in your back pocket as a last resort.

Set a deadline: If someone can't help you at the time, push for a reasonable deadline. This date should give the company sufficient time in which to make amends, without causing you undue inconvenience. Tell them that if you do not hear from them by the agreed date, you will be in contact to let them know that your complaint will go to a higher level within the organization, or to an external regulator.

Tell them the whole story: I don't advocate telling lies to garner sympathy, but sometimes you can gain some leverage by explaining how and why your particular circumstances mean that a speedy resolution is really important. For example, if your grandfather's new hearing aid breaks just days before his grandson's graduation, there's a chance that the thought of a proud, elderly man being unable to appreciate a highlight in his grandson's life might just encourage a customer service employee to be a little more helpful.

Combine two or more strategies: A couple of years ago, my friend Sean ordered a beautiful diamond ring for his wife. He intended to give it to her as a 30th birthday gift, and had made it all the more special by having it engraved with a heartfelt message on the inside of the band. Sean stopped by the jewelry store on his way home from work one evening to pick it up. He opened the box, delighted with what he saw – until he checked the engraving. He was upset to find that the jeweler had spelled his wife's name incorrectly. Obviously, he couldn't give it to her until it was fixed.

Sean immediately pointed out the error. At first, the sales clerk tried to convince Sean that he must have misspelled his own wife's name on the order form. Fortunately, Sean had taken a photo on his phone for his own records, and could quickly prove the clerk wrong. He then asked how long it would take for the jeweler to redo the engraving. The assistant store manager, who had been listening in, said that it would take roughly two or three weeks.

Sean's wife's birthday was only a week away, so he couldn't afford to wait that long. He decided to change tack. "You know," Sean said, "I chose you because you're meant to be the best jeweler in town. Perhaps I was wrong." He waited a moment. "My wife only had a basic diamond ring when we got engaged. I got this ring to make it up to her, y'know? It's a milestone birthday for her, too." After a brief silence, the assistant manager suddenly decided that the engraving could be adjusted within five days. Sean had used two strategies – mentioning the company's reputation, plus throwing in a personal story – to good effect. Complaining is an art form. Stay calm, tailor your plan of attack to the situation, and there's no reason why you can't get what you want.

Chapter 17: How To Have A Great Conversation On The Phone

Email, instant messaging, and video calls are all popular means of communication, but there is a still a place for good old-fashioned phone calls. In many respects, the principles involved in having a productive conversation are the same that apply to face-to-face interactions. For example, whether speaking in person or on the phone, you need to listen attentively, know how to deliver a sincere compliment, and create rapport.

However, the phone presents a special set of challenges. Obviously, you can't see someone's face when talking to them on the phone – there is less intimacy compared with traditional conversation. Luckily, you can learn how to use the phone to your advantage. These simple strategies will help you enjoy productive, positive conversations.

Get a reading on their availability: If you are the one placing the call (and you haven't been given a specific time to do so), always begin by asking the other person whether they have time to talk. When you start talking to someone in a regular, face-to-face setting, you usually have enough contextual information to appreciate whether or not they will be receptive to holding a conversation. On the phone, there is no way of knowing unless you ask! You should also give them an idea as to how long the call will last. Be honest. Don't pretend that your question will only take two minutes to answer if you really need an hour to discuss the problem. Give the other person a chance to make an informed decision as to how they will spend their time.

Compensate with words: When you talk with someone on the phone, they cannot see your face or physical gestures. This is an important point, because we usually draw on these cues in conversation to ascertain how someone else is feeling. So if someone cannot see your face, what should you do instead? Use your words, of course![74]

For example, let's say that your friend calls you up to tell you about their latest date – a guy they thought was very attractive and intelligent. However, once they actually started talking

---

[74] Lowndes, L. (1997). *How To Talk To Anyone*. Glasgow: Onmia Books Ltd.

to this man over dinner, it turned out he was an absolute bore who could barely make eye contact. This news might come as a surprise to you, but your friend won't be able to tell from your facial expression. A simple exclamation such as, "That's surprising!" would convey your reaction.

Single words and brief phrases such as, "I see," "I get it," and "Really? OK" are the verbal equivalent of nodding. Monitor your gestures and shifts in body language, and translate them into words. For example, if you are smiling at a witty remark your friend or colleague has made, say so. Another useful trick is work the person's name into conversation more often than you would in face-to-face interactions. It goes some way in compensating for the lack of face-to-face intimacy, and also catches their attention.

Pay attention to background noise: Be sensitive to the fact that the other person might experience interruptions. If you are calling someone at work and you hear another phone start to ring, or someone else saying their name, acknowledge the interruption and ask if they would rather continue the conversation another time. Most people will choose to carry on the conversation (arranging a time to call back is often more hassle, and they will probably want to find out what you have to say), but they will still appreciate your good manners. Remember that you are not the center of the universe, and that other people can't always predict when something (or someone) else will come up.

Cut the ramble: Opening a phone call with a polite enquiry after someone's health or their well-being in general is fine, but rambling on for several minutes will just annoy them. When we talk to someone in person, we take in their face, their posture, and their gestures – there is plenty to grab our attention. Not only that, but if we start to multitask or get distracted, it becomes pretty obvious. On the phone, all we have is a voice – and we can turn our attention elsewhere and get away with it. Don't drone on about irrelevant topics, because your conversation partner will soon focus their attention elsewhere. Establish early on what it is you want to talk about, then stay on topic.

Don't establish yourself as a negative caller: There are certain individuals – who shall remain anonymous for the sake of this book – who cause my stomach to drop whenever I see their names flash up on my phone. Why? Because whenever they call, it's always because they have some complaint to make, or because they want to use me as a sounding board for all their problems. Often, I let the call go straight to voicemail. It's a shame, because we are both missing out on the chance to have some constructive conversations, but I just don't need their negativity in my life.

Don't let yourself become one of those people who find themselves going to voicemail. Unless it's an emergency, never open with a complaint. If you approach someone in person and start talking, they have to make an effort to excuse themselves if necessary. However, if you call, they can just elect not to answer. This means that the stakes are higher when you talk to people on the phone. The impression you give will have a significant impact on the way they will deal with you in the future, if they choose to answer your calls in the first place.

Even if you have been discussing serious matters, show that you are willing to look at the situation in the best possible light. **End every call on a high note.** This may be as simple as expressing confidence that everything will work out for the best, or reminding the other person of what is going well in other areas of their life.

When leaving a message, end it on a cliffhanger: How do you get someone to call you back? There are two main points to bear in mind. First, make sure that your tone is warm and friendly. If someone has failed to pick up your call, despite telling you to get in touch at a particular time or on a particular day, you might feel irritated. However, on no account should you let this become apparent in your tone of voice. Stay calm and professional! Second, you should grab the listener's attention with a cliffhanger. Be specific.[75] "Hi, I have the figures you asked for, please call me back to hear them!" will virtually guarantee that you will receive a return call, whereas "Here are the figures you asked for:…" probably won't.

Record your most important conversations: There are several apps available that allow you to keep an audio record of your calls. Why would you want to do this? Because if someone is giving you a lot of information, you'll be able to listen to what they have to say without

---

[75] Seid, S. (2012). *8 Telephone Etiquette Tips.* advancedetiquette.com

worrying whether you have accurately recorded it on a piece of paper. You won't have to interrupt them either, or ask them to repeat themselves. This trick makes you look efficient and professional.

I'll show you an example of how this can work. My friend Sarah always records her calls whenever possible. As a marketing assistant at a large firm, her manager often calls her with information about upcoming trade shows. (For some reason, her manager prefers not to bother sending emails, but that's another story.) This information can be pretty complex, and Sarah is often bombarded with names, dates, and addresses. However, because she records calls with her manager, she never has to worry about missing a beat. As a result, everyone in her department is impressed by her superhuman memory and attention to detail. She hasn't yet revealed her secret! I'm confident that Sarah's professional approach will take her far – it makes her appear more productive than her colleagues.

Of course, you should make sure that recording your phone calls is legal in your state. As of 2017, most states allow one-party recording – as long as one party is aware that the call is being recorded (in this case, that's you), it's fine to record the conversation. However, in California, Florida, Connecticut, Illinois, Maryland, Montana, Massachusetts, New Hampshire, Pennsylvania, and Washington, you need the consent of all parties involved. Double-check the laws that apply to your state before recording without the other person's explicit consent.[76] This strategy will still impress people even if you have to ask permission, because it shows that you are taking whatever they have to say very seriously.

Send a follow-up summary: One disadvantage of holding a conversation over the phone rather than in person is that it doesn't automatically leave behind a paper trail. Recording conversations provides you with evidence that someone made a verbal commitment or particular remark, but bringing up recordings as a means of proving someone's intentions at a later date will appear hostile. It's better to write a short summary of the points addressed in the call, together with actionable steps, and send it to the other person soon after the call has ended. State in the email that unless you hear to the contrary, you will assume that your interpretation

---

[76] Digital Media Law Project. (2017). *Recording Phone Calls and Conversations.* dmlp.org

of the situation is correct.

I have focused on business calls in this section, but you can also use these tips in your personal life. For example, your friends and relatives will always appreciate it if you ask them whether they can spare a few minutes to talk. Whatever your relationship to the person on the other end of the phone, use your words to paint a picture of your responses. The phone can be an excellent tool for building a relationship if used properly, but you need to be aware of its limitations.

Chapter 18: Tips For Conversations With Non-Native Speakers

In our increasingly globalized world, conversations between native and non-native English speakers have become common in the workplace. This can present a few problems, and it can give rise to some awkward situations. A lot of my clients work in multinational corporations, and therefore interact with people from around the world. Quite often, they ask me for tips on how to have productive, mutually enjoyable conversations with their colleagues who use English as a second (or third!) language.

Don't Yell

For some reason, many of us think that by speaking at a higher volume, we will help someone else understand what we are saying. This makes no sense whatsoever. Unless you need to call out to someone who is standing on the opposite side of the room, yelling will do no good at all. In fact, it's a really bad idea. When you talk loudly to a non-native speaker, you will come across as patronizing. That's not the impression you want to give. Just speak at the same volume you would use in any other situation. There's one exception to this rule. If you are often told that you are an especially soft or quiet speaker, raise your volume a little.

Use Proper English

People who have learned English as a foreign language have usually learned "standard English." This means that they will understand you better when you use correct grammar, pronounce words as they should be spoken, and avoid slurring two or more words together. For example, "Would you like a coffee?" will be much easier for a non-native speaker to understand than, "Do-ya-wanna-coffee?"

Avoid phrases or colloquialisms specific to your geographical region, unless they are essential in conveying your meaning. In general, it's best to use short, simple words that come up frequently in everyday use. Take your lead from the non-native speaker. If they show themselves to be capable of using more advanced or unusual vocabulary, you can adjust your speech accordingly.

Filler language such as "Um, yeah," "OK, I get it," and "Literally, they…" can confuse non-native speakers, particularly if they are relatively new to using English. Filler words and phrases add no real meaning to a conversation, so don't confuse someone by sprinkling them liberally throughout your dialogue.

Watch out for "likes." Not only will you annoy native English speakers when you say "like" every ten seconds, but you will baffle people who have learned English as a second language. Overusing "like" suggests that you have poor social skills, that you have no idea how to conduct yourself in a professional environment, and that you have no confidence in what you are saying. Someone who has learned English from scratch and achieved a position of authority will think that you are an idiot! "Totally" and "Oh-my-God" are other fillers to eliminate from your speech.

Answer questions in a direct manner. When you mean "Yes," say, "Yes." When you mean "No," say, "No." Using noises and utterances such as "Uh-huh" will only add to the non-native speaker's confusion.

It's usually best to use long forms rather than contractions. This is because non-native speakers often have problems distinguishing between a word and related contractions. For example, the difference between "should" and "shouldn't" is subtle for a non-native speaker. This can all too easily result in misunderstandings.

Be Aware Of The Broader Context

If a non-native speaker doesn't understand you, it may seem obvious that the language barrier is to blame. However, you need to appreciate that other factors might be at work.[77] Cultural barriers and expectations as to how people interact with one another might be to blame for miscommunication. For example, if one speaker is from a culture that values a direct style of communication, whereas their conversation partner grew up in a culture that uses subtle hints rather than direct commands, there is scope for misunderstandings that actually have nothing to do with language. If you aren't certain whether a miscommunication is down to

---

77 Cultural Awareness International. (2013). *Communicating Effectively With Non-Native English Speakers.* culturalawareness.com

language, and the other person is from a different culture, a bit of background reading could help you figure out what is going on. You should also consider whether your miscommunication might have arisen as a result of differences in age, gender, and prior experience of working within other company cultures.

Other Tips To Make Communication Easier

Repeat, then rephrase if necessary: When a native speaker doesn't appear to understand you, your first instinct is probably to repeat what you have just said. Do the same with a non-native speaker, because they may not have misunderstood – they might have simply failed to hear every word. If they don't understand you the second time around, rephrase the sentence, replacing the most complex words with simpler terms. Repeat the whole sentence every time until they get the message. This might be more time consuming than repeating one or two key words, but it will be less confusing for the non-native speaker.

Give the speaker a fair chance to respond: If you speak a language other than your native tongue, you'll know that formulating a grammatically correct response can take a few seconds longer than usual. Bear this in mind when talking to a non-native speaker.

Ask someone to rephrase what you said in their own words: Instead of asking, "Do you understand what I just said?" ask them, "Can you tell me what you think I said?" This will let you clear up any misunderstandings early on.

Unless you are asked to do so, do not correct the speaker: When someone wants to learn English, they attend lessons with a teacher, or they make a point of asking those around them to offer corrections if they make a mistake. Resist the urge to leap in and tell them where they are going wrong. They might appreciate your input, but it's more likely that they will be embarrassed or offended.

Minimize your use of words that mean different things across contexts: There are many words in the English language that carry various meanings depending on the way in which they are used. This creates conditions that may give rise to misunderstandings. For example, suppose you tell a non-native speaker that there was a meeting "last Monday." They may think you meant that the meeting in question took place on the final Monday (perhaps of the month), because "last" can mean the same thing as "final" in some contexts. It would be better to say, "There was a meeting X days ago," or "There was a meeting on [date]."

Make your questions direct, with no preamble: If you have a habit of building up to a question with phrases such as, "If it's not too much trouble, I was wondering…" or "I'd like you to…," streamline your requests! "Please can you do X?" or "Would you be able to do Y?" will be less confusing for the other person.

Use the active tense: The active tense is usually easier to understand as compared to the passive tense. For example, "Company X sold that product" will be less confusing than, "The product was sold by Company X."[78]

Keep a piece of paper and a pen to hand: Despite your best efforts, there may still be occasions on which you can't get your message across. This might be because you are using specific jargon, because you have a very thick accent, or the non-native speaker just doesn't have the vocabulary required to understand what you mean. This is where diagrams come in to play. It's sensible to write down complex instructions if it's essential that the non-native speaker follows them to the letter.

Make use of gestures and facial expressions: Body language can provide useful contextual cues. Although people of different cultures vary in terms of what gestures they find distasteful, or the extent to which they believe public displays of emotion to be acceptable, most psychologists agree that almost everyone can recognize happiness, sadness, disgust, and fear. You don't have to exaggerate your facial expressions and gestures, but there's no harm in consciously making sure that your nonverbal cues are reflecting the words coming from your mouth.

Think carefully before using humor: Humor can be hard to pull off in a corporate setting

---

[78] Marshall, L.B. (2015). *Tips for Talking with Non-Native English Speakers.* quickanddirtytips.com

at the best of times. Throw language barriers and cultural differences into the mix, and you have a recipe for potential disaster.[79] Instead of making jokes, use friendly body language to put the speaker at ease. If it turns out that the language barrier is not as significant as you imagined, you can use humor once you have built come to know the other person a little better.

Give a non-native speaker every reasonable chance to prepare for important conversations: When preparing for a meeting with a non-native speaker, give them a clear agenda in advance. Keep the language simple. If you must use jargon or acronyms that are alien to the non-native speaker, make sure that the document contains a glossary.

If you don't understand the speaker, use "I" language: Imagine that you are trying to speak in a foreign language, and struggling to make yourself understood. Which would you rather hear – "Sorry, you'll need to say that again," or "I'm sorry, I didn't understand that"? When misunderstandings arise, take some of the blame. Emphasize that part of the problem is your own failure to comprehend what they are saying. This will help the speaker feel less self-conscious.[80]

Always treat a non-native speaker with respect. If you have ever learned another language, you'll know how challenging it can be to achieve fluency. Don't be too quick to judge someone's personality or intellect based on the quality of their conversation, because they may well be more expressive and better able to voice their thoughts in their native language.

---

[79] Bell, N.D. (2007). How native and non-native English speakers adapt to humor in intercultural interaction. *Humor, 20,* 27-48.
[80] Ibid.

Chapter 19: How To Put Your Views Across To Someone In Authority

So far in this book, I've assumed that you and your conversation partner are pretty much equal in terms of authority and power. However, as the emails I've had from my readers show, some of the hardest conversations we ever have are with those in positions of authority. It's doubly difficult when you want to give your views – which might even go against what the authority figure happens to believe – without risking your reputation or job.

Here's how you can make yourself heard without appearing disrespectful:

Assume that they will be open to working with you: Authority figures are there to do a job, and most of them take pride in their interpersonal skills. Some bosses are complete nightmares – I wouldn't deny it! But, in my experience, most people in senior management positions are easy to work with when you treat them with respect. Don't assume that they won't want to hear what you have to say just because they have a lot more knowledge and experience. It's actually quite annoying, even awkward, to watch someone grovel at your feet. They were once in your position, and they probably haven't forgotten what it was like to feel nervous when standing in front of those in more senior roles. Even if they don't go out of their way to help you feel comfortable, they might be more empathetic than you first realize.

If you disagree, say so: The best communicators respect someone who is willing to put their opinions forward. When you are asked for your honest feedback, give it. Remain polite and diplomatic, but tell them what's really on your mind. Think of it this way – if your boss asks you for your opinion and you give them a simple, "Yes, of course, whatever you say, Boss!" they aren't going to think very highly of you. Such answers are just a waste of everyone's time.

Use the "praise sandwich" or "positivity sandwich" technique: If an authority figure asks for your feedback and you need to break some bad news, use the sandwich technique. Begin with a brief positive remark, deliver your negative feedback, then finish on a high. For example, let's say that you have been asked to give feedback on how your department is performing. You might say something like, "The sales figures are up this quarter, which is great. Unfortunately, our customer satisfaction has dropped by ten per cent. To address this, we are investing in a new training program." Always take responsibility where appropriate.

Ask questions that show your respect for their authority: Going into interview mode isn't a good idea, but sneaking a couple of questions that acknowledge their expertise and authority is a subtle way of showing that you hold them in esteem. Asking questions like, "Whilst you're here, could I ask for your opinion on X technology?" or "I heard you went to Trade Show Y last week – how was it?" show that you are mindful of their knowledge and experience. If you are dealing with an authority figure with a fragile ego, this tactic will reassure them that you recognize who's boss.

Keep your body language assertive: Remember that authority figures are just people! They might have a special title or enjoy a great deal of status, but they are still vulnerable human beings with their unique strengths and weaknesses.[81] Remind yourself that they are in no way intrinsically "better" than you – it will show in your body language and overall level of confidence. Self-assured, successful people respect others who carry themselves with dignity.

Brace yourself for criticism, and thank them for their feedback: The average authority figure has to provide feedback – both positive and negative – as part of their job. The golden rule is to avoid taking it personally. Remember that unless you are an extremely small organization, they are unlikely to know you as an individual. Even if they use an unpleasant tone of voice or make snide remarks, it's your work that they dislike, not you. If they deliver negative feedback, thank them! Let them know that it will help you perform at a higher level. Make it clear that you understand why they are dissatisfied, and that it is your responsibility to improve your own performance. Do not become defensive.[82] Tell them that you look forward to making changes. You will gain a reputation as a mature, professional individual who values your self-development over your ego.

Stand up for yourself when necessary: There is no need to take the blame for something you didn't do, or to agree when someone makes unfair accusations against you, even if the

---

[81] Social Anxiety Home. (2017). *Fear of Authority Figures: 7 Tips on How to Talk to Authority Figures.* socialanxietyhome.com
[82] WikiHow. (2017). *How To Talk To Authority.* wikihow.com

accuser is in a position of authority. At the same time, becoming angry or hysterical will not help the situation. If someone accuses you of something you didn't do, say, "I know this is a very serious situation, but I did not do that. I don't know what you are talking about." I won't deny that it's scary to stand up to authority figures, but remind yourself that telling the truth is usually the best course of action. After all, you wouldn't want to lie to them, would you? One way or another, the truth usually comes out in the end. If you stood up to the authority figure at the time, they will respect you. If they never accept the real story and keep blaming you for something you did not do, then you can at least rest assured that you did all you could in telling them what really happened. Your personal integrity will remain intact.

Watch out for rhetorical questions: People in authority often use rhetorical questions as a means of asserting their power. These include, "What are we supposed to do now?," and "How I am meant to turn this around?" They create a dramatic atmosphere, and can also give them a few extra seconds in which to process their thoughts. They are not intended as an invitation for others to speak. Answering a rhetorical question will make you appear overly confident and socially naïve.[83] For example, suppose that you have been called in to speak to your boss because your team has failed to meet an important project deadline. If your boss says, "How could it have all gone so wrong?, What am I supposed to tell the Board?" you should realize that this isn't an invitation for you to tell him how to do his job! If, however, your boss says, "What do you have to say about that?," then it's time to tell him your thoughts.

If you are nervous about a meeting or appointment with an authority figure, take an advocate with you: Ideally, you will be able to draw on your conversation skills when talking to someone in authority. However, if you are faced with the prospect of a tense meeting, you may want to take someone along for support. For example, if you have been told to attend a meeting with a senior manager at work in order to receive a formal warning, ask HR whether you can take an advocate or representative with you. If you need to attend a doctor's appointment but are afraid that you won't be able to talk about a personal or embarrassing problem, take a trusted friend or relative along.

---

[83] Ibid.

If you find yourself crippled by anxiety, get help: It's normal to be apprehensive when meeting with someone in authority. However, if you find yourself having panic attacks at the thought of talking to someone in power, it might be time to consider getting professional help. This is because a strong fear of authority figures is often linked to other issues, such as social anxiety or unresolved issues with child-parent relationships.[84] The good news is that even severe cases of social anxiety can be resolved with the right help and support.

---

[84] Anxiety Boss. (2015). *I Get Extremely Anxious When I'm Talking To Someone Of Authority.* anxietyboss.com

Chapter 20: Conversations Between Hearing & Hearing Impaired Individuals

Did you know that 48 million Americans live with significant hearing loss?[85] There's a good chance that you either know, or work with, someone who has a hearing impairment – or perhaps you are an individual living with hearing loss. Either way, it can make communication difficult. Hearing loss is associated with social embarrassment and general isolation, because those afflicted often struggle to follow everyday conversations.[86]

If you have a hearing impairment, these tips will help you enjoy more productive conversations:

Ask people to stand or sit in a position that works for you: If you hear better on one side than the other, either move so that you have a better chance of understanding what someone is saying, or tell them that you have a hearing impairment and you would appreciate it if they could speak from one side rather than the other.

In general, it is a good idea to let your conversation partner know as soon as possible that you have a hearing impairment, and the exact steps they can take to help you. Tell them that following a conversation is easier for you if they keep their hands away from their mouths, speak clearly, and so forth. Don't hide your impairment – a well-mannered person will do everything they reasonably can to accommodate you.

Locate specific sources of difficulty, and give positive instructions: If you are having trouble understanding a particular individual, think why this might be. You can then make a proactive request that will make the conversation easier for everyone.[87] For example, if you realize that your conversation partner speaks unusually quickly, you could ask, "Please could you speak a little more slowly?"

Find an alternative to "what?": It isn't your fault that you cannot hear clearly, but saying

---

85 Hearing Loss Association of America. (2017). *Hearing Loss: Facts & Statistics*. hearingloss.org
86 Athens Hearing & Balance Clinic. (2017). *Effects of Hearing Loss*. athenshearing.com
87 Kricos, P.B. (2017). *Communication Strategies*. betterhearing.org

"What?" throughout the conversation may still appear rude.[88] "Could you please repeat that?," "Sorry, I didn't catch that," and "Pardon?" are all better alternatives.

Use suitable clarifying questions: If you heard part of a sentence but didn't catch a couple of words, ask for clarification using questions that show you were listening to the best of your ability. For example, suppose you are talking to someone who is telling you about their new house. You understood that they purchased the house recently, and that they have painted the living room, but you didn't catch the color scheme they used. Rather than saying "Pardon?" - this could be taken as an instruction to repeat the entire sentence - you could say, "OK, I got that you have painted the living room, but not the color scheme. Could you repeat that?"

Repeat back important details: If someone has given you some essential information, say, "I want to make sure I understand this. May I repeat it back?" Your conversation partner will be glad that you have taken the initiative.

Suggest a "talking stick:" Keeping up with a conversation as part of a group is often difficult for a person with a hearing impairment, because the normal flow of interruptions and crosstalk can be too hard to decipher. If this is a problem for you, and you have a good relationship with the group in question, suggest that the group uses an aid to minimize interruptions.

The "talking stick" doesn't have to literally be a stick – it can be any small object, such as a mug. The rule is that someone can only talk when they are holding the object. As a person with a hearing impairment, the "stick" will direct your attention to the right person and help you follow the conversation.

What can hearing people do to facilitate smooth conversations with someone with a hearing impairment? Following these guidelines is a good start:

Understand how hearing aids work: Most people assume that hearing aids work in

---

[88] Booth, S. (2017). *Hearing Loss: Tips for Better Communication.* webmd.com

much the same way as a pair of glasses. When someone puts on their spectacles, their vision is completely restored. This isn't the case with hearing aids. Aids amplify the sounds someone can hear, but they don't always make those sounds clearer. Do not assume that someone can hear "normally" just because they are wearing a hearing aid.[89]

Get their attention first: Before launching into conversation, say the person's name. Wait until you have their attention, and then start talking. This approach reduces the likelihood that they will miss the beginning of a sentence.

Do not shout: Although it sounds counterintuitive, raising your voice can actually make it harder for someone to understand you, because it distorts your speech. Speak at your usual volume.[90]

Face them and keep your mouth uncovered: Not all people with hearing loss have learned how to lip read. However, most will typically rely on recognition of common mouth shapes to help them understand what is being said. Ensure they can see your mouth at all times. Do not attempt to talk to them from another room.[91] Move to a well-lit space if necessary. Sit between three and six feet away from the person.

Spell out a word if necessary: If you have repeated a word a couple of times, but the other person doesn't appear to have understood, spell it out. Keep a piece of paper and a pen to hand in case you can't communicate what you need to say.

Ask whether one ear is more functional than the other: A person's hearing loss may not be symmetrical. Quite often, they will hear better in one ear than the other. If it's appropriate to do so, ask them whether they will be able to hear you better if you sit in a particular position.

Be prepared to rephrase or reword what you are saying: Sometimes, a person may find it hard to discern specific sounds. This means that they might find it difficult to comprehend

---

[89] Eberts, S. (2016). *Ten Reasons Hearing Aids Are NOT Like Glasses.* livingwithhearingloss.com
[90] UCSF Medical Center. (2017). *Communicating with People with Hearing Loss.* ucsfhealth.org
[91] Ibid.

certain words or phrases. If they look puzzled, try a different word or expression instead.

Ask them to repeat key pieces of information back to you: Even people who have intact hearing capabilities can confuse two words that sound alike. When you are giving someone with hearing loss names, dates, numbers, or times, ask them to repeat them back to you. Be sure to phrase your request politely, so that they don't feel as though you are patronizing them. For example, you could ask, "You probably heard that, but could you repeat it, just for my peace of mind?"

Take your share of responsibility for any misunderstandings: Despite your best efforts, you might encounter an embarrassing or awkward misunderstanding. If this happens, be prepared to laugh at yourself and the situation – never at the person with hearing loss. Assure them that you will try to communicate more clearly in the future. Always show courtesy. Never talk about a person with a hearing impairment as though they are not in the room – this is extremely rude. If you are in a group situation and the topic under discussion suddenly changes, pause a moment to make sure that the person with a hearing impairment has caught up. You should minimize crosstalk and interruptions. If possible, provide the person with an overview of what the discussion will cover ahead of time. This will provide them with contextual clues.

Chapter 21: How To Excel In Interviews & Get That Job

It's no secret that people with strong interpersonal skills are more likely to be hired. In fact, the ability to hold a conversation and speak calmly under pressure can even go some way in compensating for a lack of experience and qualifications. Why? Because an interview allows you to show not only why your skills make you a strong candidate for the position, but it also lets you demonstrate that you have sufficient social intelligence to function within the workplace.

What's The Point Of An Interview, Anyway?

Before jumping into conversation tips for interviews, let's review your aims as an applicant. First, you need to work out whether you are a good fit for the organization. You should always read up on the company culture prior to making an application, but attending an interview allows you another level of insight into how the organization is run. For example, if the interviewer appears unprepared or nervous, this tells you a few things about their training practices! Unless you are in dire need of a job, move out of the "I'll accept any offer I can get!" mentality. Instead, reframe an interview as an opportunity for both parties to see whether a job offer would be appropriate. I always tell my clients that making this switch is essential if you want to remain calm throughout the process. Calm people make for better conversationalists.

Your second objective is to show the interviewer that you have the qualifications, experience, and personal qualities required for the job. This will require you to speak in a succinct manner that communicates your main points, without appearing brusque or arrogant. Interviewers usually ask competency-based questions too, and these require strong listening skills and a clear head (plus some advance preparation). It isn't enough to just rattle off the contents of your resume. If you really want to impress an interviewer and land the job, you need to build rapport. These tips will help you do just that:

Don't slow your speech: Well-meaning teachers and parents might have told you, "Slow down, or you'll appear nervous!" Actually, research conducted with over 100 students in mock interview situations has shown that slow speakers come across as anxious. Speak at your usual pace.[92]

Cut the filler: Few verbal tics undermine your credibility faster than fillers such as "um," "erm," and "y'know." They are distracting, and the interviewer might even struggle to focus on the points you are trying to make! Fillers also make you appear shy and unsure of yourself. In the days leading up to an interview, pay attention to the number of filler words you tend to use when talking to others. Work on cutting them down. Ideally, you should eliminate them altogether. Career expert Jayne Latz advises that you should use no more than one filler word per minute.[93] If you need to pause during an interview, ask for a moment to gather your thoughts, or buy yourself a few seconds by asking the interviewer to repeat the question. It's better than going, "Um...ahhh..." and so on.

Watch your intonation: I've never heard someone tell me that they enjoy talking to someone who uses an upward inflection at the end of every sentence. To create an impression of confidence, only speak with a raised pitch if you are actually asking a question.[94] When making a statement, deliver it as though you have no doubt that what you are saying is correct.

Don't qualify your statements: If someone told you, "I'm hoping to achieve my MBA within the next five years," or "I think I'll take a vacation in Italy," part of you will doubt that they really believe in their own goals. On the other hand, if someone said, "I'm going to achieve my MBA within the next five years," or "I am going to Italy," you would be more likely to believe them. The same principle applies in job interviews. Use words like "hopefully," "perhaps," and "sort of" sparingly. If you are going to make a point, make it with conviction! "Weak speak" suggests that you are lacking in self-belief, which is not an attractive quality in a job candidate.[95]

Marry together confidence and enthusiasm: Interviewers really like a candidate who is both qualified for the role and enthusiastic about their career. Public speaking coach Holley Murchison recommends a simple recipe for success based on this principle. Prior to the interview, make a list. It should contain all the reasons why you know that you can perform the

---

[92] Shoemaker, N. (2016). *How You Speak Matters Most During Job Interviews.* bigthink.com
[93] Latz, J. (2010). *4 Steps to Speak Better in Interviews.* theladders.com
[94] Diresta, D. (2017). *Six Sloppy Speech Habits.* monster.com
[95] Ibid.

job. In other words, it should remind you why you are capable. The next step is to move through each item, devising a reason why each competency inspires you, or makes you feel enthusiastic about the work.[96] This preparation will help you answer any questions about your skills and competence. Pairing confidence and enthusiasm will help you generate strong statements like this:

"In my 10 years as a HR consultant, I have learned how to create convincing, engaging presentations. This skill has helped me communicate key ideas to employees across a number of sectors, but the most rewarding part is using this ability to engage with workers in devising solutions to common HR problems."

Stick to the 60-second rule: Long-winded answers will not endear you to the interviewer. To be blunt, if you can't answer an interview question in under a minute, you need to rethink your approach. Run a search on the most popular interview questions, and ensure you could put together a good response within one minute.[97]

Use "we" language along with "I": Very few jobs require a worker to carry out their duties in isolation. An interviewer will want reassurance that you are capable of working both independently and as part of a team. A good way of communicating that you have both abilities is to use both "I" and "we" language. For example:

"In our department, we always make a point of getting our projects completed in advance of the deadline. I have taken responsibility for scheduling my team's working hours using our in-house time management software. Our most recent project was delivered a week ahead of the deadline."

In summary, you need to communicate to your interviewer what it is that you do, and the ways in which you work with others to meet your team's goals.[98]

---

[96] Murchison, H. (2013). *5 Public Speaking Tips That'll Prepare You for Any Interview*. mashable.com
[97] Ibid.
[98] Ibid.

Make friendly small talk: I've already told you why small talk is such a useful social tool, and my small talk tips also apply in interview situations. If the interviewer is escorting you to an interview room, they will probably try to engage you in small talk. This is actually part of the interview process – they want to see how you function in high-pressure social situations. Make a good first impression by engaging with the interviewer. Don't make them do all the work to keep the conversation alive! If you have to talk to a receptionist or administrator before your interview, be sure to make a good impression on them too. You never know, the interviewer might just be good friends with the man or woman on the front desk. In addition, if you do get the job, you will want to start your working relationship off on the right foot.

How To Handle Those Awkward Interview Questions

After graduating college, I started lining up interviews for my first professional, full-time job. When I applied for a role within a company, I always took the time to read up on the organization's history, culture, goals, and recent performance. I took the advice of my college's career center, and prepared answers to common interview questions. Sounds good, doesn't it? Unfortunately, I was far too arrogant, and I was about to learn a valuable lesson the hard way!

I arrived early to my first interview. A few minutes later, my interviewer came into the lobby, greeted me warmly, and started walking me to the interview room. As she hung her jacket on the back of the door, she said, "So, tell me about yourself!" I opened my mouth to reply – but nothing came out. Did I know that someone would ask me that question? Absolutely. Had I prepared? Nope. My young, naïve self assumed that of course I would be able to think up an answer on the spot – after all, I knew who I was, right? I can't even remember what I said, but I can tell you that I didn't get the job. The moral of the story? Always prepare, however smart or self-aware you might be. There's something about a job interview that causes even the best conversationalists to panic.

I'm not going to list every conceivable question an interviewer might ask you. There are lots of lists available for free online. Not only that, but according to career experts, there are only a few types of question you need to prepare for anyway.[99] Consider the following:[100]

"So why do you want this job?" The interviewer knows full well that most people work because they need the money, not because they really love what they do. However, this question is helpful for weeding out applicants who haven't bothered to do their homework. You should give an answer that proves you have thought about why the role is right for you. There are several ways you can do this. You might tell the interviewer what it is you admire about the company, you might describe what aspects of the job advertisement caught your eye, or (if you have a background in another industry) why you want to change careers at this point in your life. Make sure you know the company's history, the products and services they offer, their core values, their mission, their organizational structure, their recent successes and challenges, and where they hope to go in the future. All this information will be available online, primarily through their website. No one will believe you are serious about the job if you haven't even bothered to read up on the organization.

"What are your strengths?" Interviewers ask this question in an attempt to work out whether your capabilities will be a good fit for the role. This is no time for modesty! You should be able to talk about two or three competencies that would make you suitable for the job. Do not give generic answers that suggest you can only meet the bare minimum standards of job performance (e.g. "I always show up to work on time!"). Instead, hone in on what makes you a unique, valuable candidate. You should also be able to give **at least one** recent example of how you used these skills to good effect.

"What are your weaknesses?" Some well-meaning career advisors will tell you that you should take a positive trait (e.g. perfectionism) and frame it as a negative (e.g. "I've been told I'm too much of a perfectionist!"). This is an overused tactic, and it will only make the interviewer want to roll their eyes. Instead, be honest without ruining your chances. Choose a relatively minor weakness that can be corrected with the right practice and training, such as a mild fear of public speaking.[101]

---

[99] Sundberg, J. (2017). *The Only 5 Interview Questions You Need to Prepare for*. theundercoverrecruiter.com
[100] Young, J. (2017). *The Top 5 Interview Questions to Practice*. theundercoverrecruiter.com
[101] Ibid.

"What can you bring to the organization?" This question is actually a gift. It's a direct invitation to sell yourself. Prepare a brief summary of your key skills, along with a description of how they can benefit the organization. Note that it isn't enough to just list your main achievements. You need to put them into context. See the example below:

BAD: "I'm a hard worker and a good team leader, so I'll be able to help your business grow."
GOOD: "I'm a hard worker, which led to my appointment as team leader last year. Since then, our profits have increased by thirty per cent. I would love the opportunity to bring these skills to your organization."

"Where would you like to be five years from now?" The answer you give to this question needs to suggest that you have given some thought to your career trajectory, and that you have applied for a particular role as a means of working towards your ambitions. Talk about the kind of position you would like to take on within your industry, but don't forget to mention the skills you want to pick up along the way. This will give the interviewer the impression that you aren't just looking for status and money – it suggests that you are interested in broadening your skill set.

"What are your expectations with regards to salary?" The best response to this question requires a little preparation, but it's worth it. Spend half an hour on Google looking up the average salary for someone of your experience within your industry, and come up with a realistic salary bracket that takes this information into account. You can also look at other advertised jobs from similar companies – if they give salary information, this is another useful marker.

What Do You Do When It's Your Turn To Ask The Questions?

Towards the end of the interview, you will usually be asked, "And do you have any questions for me?" Your answer should always be, "Yes!" A candidate who just says, "No, everything sounds fine" has wasted an opportunity to show the interviewer that they are really engaging with the process.
Questions relating to training and development opportunities are usually a good bet. "What

training will be available to me?" and "Are there many opportunities to advance in the company?" both show that you care about your career, and suggest that you have really thought about what it would be like to work for the organization within a particular role. Do not ask questions about vacations, benefits, annual raises, or salary. Once an interviewer has answered your question, be sure to thank them for their time before leaving the interview room.

Tips For Phone Interviews

Most of the tips in this chapter also apply to phone interviews. However, phone interviews are often used as an initial screening tool rather than a means of making a final decision on whether to give an applicant a job. As a result, the typical phone interview will focus on your general skills and profile, with less emphasis on the specific duties contained within a particular role. You should be prepared to give brief but informative answers to the broadest interview questions such as, "Tell me a little about yourself," and "What made you apply for this role?" You will also need to convey enthusiasm. Inject more energy into your voice than you would in a traditional interview. On the phone, the interviewer cannot see your body language or facial expression, so you will need to choose your words carefully when expressing your feelings and enthusiasm for the job.

If you have to take part in a phone interview, you can take advantage of the opportunity to make notes. For those of us who get nervous during interviews – and let's face it, that's most people! – notes can act as a security blanket. However, I wouldn't recommend that you refer to notes during a phone interview. This is for two reasons. First, you can never know for sure what an interviewer will say, and trying to make any prewritten answers fit into the situation, rather than devising an answer to fit the question, will cause you to become flustered. Second, you don't want to get into the habit of relying on notes during an interview, because you won't be able to do this when meeting the interviewer in person.

Here's a final tip – even if you aren't going anywhere else that day, wear your best interviewing outfit during the interview. Our clothes have a big effect on how we feel, and professional attire can place you in a confident, business-oriented frame of mind. This will have a positive psychological effect that will show in your speech. It should go without saying that you should always address the interviewer by their title and surname until you are invited to use their first name.

Remember That Social Skills Aren't Enough

You might have a great interview, but still fail to get the job. If this happens to you, don't take it personally. An interviewer's role is to figure out whether you will be a good fit within the organization. This goes beyond your conversation skills – it's also about your personality. Sometimes, an interviewer will be looking for an extroverted person to fill a position, because that's the kind of individual a team needs at that moment in time. An introverted candidate may be able to do the job, but they might find it hard to integrate with those already working in the department.

If possible, ask for feedback following an unsuccessful job interview. You might not like reading or hearing the interviewer's answer, but accept it graciously – it could help you land a job in the future. Not only that, but if you apply for another position within the same company, you will already have established a reputation as someone who takes their personal development seriously.

Conclusion

You now have all the tools you need to take the quality of your conversations to a new level. Whether you want to improve your social life or secure a new job, your social skills play a huge role in your success. Throughout this book, I've used everyday examples and scientific studies that prove this to be true. What are you waiting for? It's time to get out there and put your knowledge into practice!

In improving your conversation skills, you'll also improve your cognitive functioning. For instance, research shows that the simple act of making small talk in the workplace can boost problem-solving and planning skills.[102] Good conversation also allows you to strengthen your social networks.[103] Your relationships will become stronger, and you'll always have people to call upon if you need help.

As your skills improve, you'll soon see the positive effects begin to manifest in every area of your life. For example, you'll no longer feel stressed when a product or service doesn't work, because you'll know how to make an effective complaint. You'll feel less stressed about moving to a new workplace or neighborhood, because you'll know how to make friends – you won't feel like an outsider.

If you need to work through a delicate issue with your boss or a difficult client, you'll know how to handle the situation. Family vacations and gatherings will be considerably less stressful when you don't have to worry about getting into the same old fights time and time again. Picking up this book might be one of the smartest moves you ever made.

In reading this guide, you've probably realized just how many people find it hard to hold a decent conversation. Why not take the initiative and help those around you improve their communication skills? If you are a manager, think about whether your team's conversation skills could do with a boost. Perhaps it's time to consider a new training program, or to assign

---

[102] Ybarra, O., Winkielman, P., Yeh, I., Burnstein, E., & Kavanagh, L. (2010). Friends (and Sometimes Enemies) With Cognitive Benefits: What Types of Social Interactions Boost Executive Functioning? *Social Psychological and Personality Science*, 1-9.
[103] Good Day At Work. (2017). *3 Reasons Why Conversation Is Important*. robertsoncooper.com

team members tasks that will allow them to develop their abilities. For example, if they usually work individually, could you find ways of encouraging more collaborative working practices? If you are in a junior role, ask your manager whether your organization offers communication skills training. If not, request that they consider doing so.

If you are a parent, take responsibility for your child's communication skills. We all know that a good education, healthy diet, and regular exercise are essential in setting a child up for a solid start in life. But how many parents ask themselves, "Is my child good at making conversation? Are they going to be able to make friends with people of different backgrounds? Are they going to feel confident walking into an interview room?" I don't think that most parents realize the importance of these skills until their child runs into problems, whether that's trouble getting along with their classmates at school, or failing to get a job after college.

The best thing you can do is model these skills. Give your child the chance to see you talk to a variety of people, and give them the opportunity to socialize with people from a range of backgrounds. Show them how to build friendships, sort out disagreements, make complaints, and argue in a constructive manner.

Some people think that arguing in front of a child is always a bad idea, but if conflict is handled well, it can actually be a good thing. If a child witnesses their parents resolving their differences without shouting, dirty tactics, insults, or abuse, they will grow up knowing that arguments aren't the end of the world.[104]

Of course, arguments about topics that aren't appropriate for children should be held in private, and frequent fights can leave a child with psychological damage. Children are highly astute. Preschool children can tell the difference between genuine resolution and fake reconciliation, so don't try and pretend that everything is fine when the problem still hasn't been solved.[105]

Self-development, combined with lots of practice, is enough to make most people into

---

[104] Divecha, D. (2014). *What Happens To Children When Parents Fight.* developmentalscience.com
[105] Ibid.

capable conversationalists. However, you might find that you are still anxious in social situations. If you feel overwhelmed by the thought of talking to people, whether at work or in your personal life, consider seeking professional help. This might take the form of counseling, or you might choose to hire a coach. You may be reluctant to spend the money, but think of it as a sensible investment in your future. If you need a reminder of why it's so important to develop sound communication skills, refer back to the introduction of this book.

On the other hand, you may discover that you have a real talent for engaging people in conversation. There are a number of ways you can take advantage of your ability. For example, you could build on your skills and learn how to become a captivating public speaker. Join an organization, such as Toastmasters International, that will support you in becoming a first-rate orator. If you work for an organization that regularly sends people to conferences and public events, start volunteering yourself as a representative. You could also offer your skills to charities – they always need engaging people to help their fundraising efforts.

I hope that this guide has been useful, and that you feel inspired to give your conversation skills an overhaul. I wish you all the best in developing your relationships, supercharging your career, and enjoying thousands of exciting conversations in the years to come! Good luck!

<u>One last thing before you go – Can I ask you a favor? I need your help!</u> If you like this book, could you please share your experience on Amazon and write an honest review? It will be just one minute for you (I will be happy even with one sentence!), but a GREAT help for me and definitely good Karma ☺. Since I'm not a well-established author and I don't have powerful people and big publishing companies supporting me, <u>I read every single review and jump around with joy like a little kid every time my readers comment on my books and give me their honest feedback!</u> If I was able to inspire you in any way, please let me know! It will also help me get my books in front of more people looking for new ideas and useful knowledge.

If you did not enjoy the book or had a problem with it, please don't hesitate to contact me at <u>contact@mindfulnessforsuccess.com</u> **and tell me how I can improve it to provide more value and more knowledge to my readers.** I'm constantly working on my books to make them better and more helpful.

Thank you and good luck! I believe in you and I wish you all the best on your new journey!

Your friend,

Ian

Don't hesitate to visit:
-My Blog: www.mindfulnessforsuccess.com
-My Facebook fanpage: https://www.facebook.com/mindfulnessforsuccess
-My Instagram profile: https://instagram.com/mindfulnessforsuccess
-My Amazon profile: amazon.com/author/iantuhovsky

My Free Gift to You – Get One of My Audiobooks For Free!

If you've never created an account on Audible (the biggest audiobook store in the world), **you can claim one free** audiobook **of mine**!

It's a simple process:

1. Pick one of my audiobooks on Audible:

http://www.audible.com/search?advsearchKeywords=Ian+Tuhovsky

2. Once you choose a book and open its detail page, click the orange button "Free with 30-Day Trial Membership."

3. Follow the instructions to create your account and download your first free audiobook.

Note that you are NOT obligated to continue after your free trial expires. You can cancel your free trial easily anytime and you won't be charged at all.

Also, if you haven't downloaded your free book already:

<u>Discover How to Get Rid of Stress & Anxiety and Reach Inner Peace in 20 Days or Less!</u>

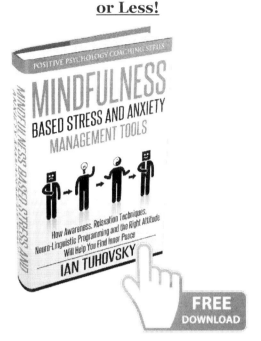

To help speed up your personal transformation, I have prepared a special gift for you!

Download my full, 120 page e-book "Mindfulness Based Stress and Anxiety Management Tools" for free <u>by clicking here.</u>

Link:

tinyurl.com/mindfulnessgift

<u>Hey there like-minded friends, let's get connected!</u>

Don't hesitate to visit:
-My Blog: www.mindfulnessforsuccess.com
-My Facebook fanpage: https://www.facebook.com/mindfulnessforsuccess
-My Instagram profile: https://instagram.com/mindfulnessforsuccess
-My Amazon profile: amazon.com/author/iantuhovsky

Recommended Reading for You

If you are interested in Self-Development, Psychology, Social Dynamics, PR, Soft Skills, Spirituality and related topics, you might be interested in previewing or downloading my other books:

Communication Skills Training: A Practical Guide to Improving Your Social Intelligence, Presentation, Persuasion and Public Speaking

Do You Know How To Communicate With People Effectively, Avoid Conflicts and Get What You Want From Life?

...It's not only about what you say, but also about WHEN, WHY and HOW you say it.

Do The Things You Usually Say Help You, Or Maybe Hold You Back?

Have you ever considered **how many times you intuitively felt that maybe you lost something important or crucial, simply because you unwittingly said or did something, which put somebody off?** Maybe it was a misfortunate word, bad formulation, inappropriate joke, forgotten name, huge misinterpretation, awkward conversation or a strange tone of your voice?
Maybe you assumed that you knew exactly what a particular concept meant for another person and you stopped asking questions?
Maybe you could not listen carefully or could not stay silent for a moment? **How many times have you wanted to achieve something, negotiate better terms, or ask for a promotion and failed miserably?**

It's time to put that to an end with the help of this book.

Lack of communication skills is exactly what ruins most peoples' lives.
If you don't know how to communicate properly, you are going to have problems both in your intimate and family relationships.

You are going to be ineffective in work and business situations. It's going to be troublesome managing employees or getting what you want from your boss or your clients on a daily basis. Overall, **effective communication is like an engine oil which makes your life run smoothly, getting you wherever you want to be.** There are very few areas in life in which you can succeed in the long run without this crucial skill.

What Will You Learn With This Book?

-What Are The **Most Common Communication Obstacles** Between People And How To Avoid Them
-How To Express Anger And Avoid Conflicts
-What Are **The Most 8 Important Questions You Should Ask Yourself** If You Want To Be An Effective Communicator?
-**5 Most Basic and Crucial** Conversational Fixes
-How To Deal With Difficult and Toxic People
-Phrases to **Purge from Your Dictionary** (And What to Substitute Them With)
-The Subtle Art of **Giving and Receiving Feedback**
-Rapport, the **Art of Excellent Communication**
-How to Use Metaphors to **Communicate Better** And **Connect With People**
-What Metaprograms and Meta Models Are and How Exactly To Make Use of Them To **Become A Polished Communicator**
-How To Read Faces and **How to Effectively Predict Future Behaviors**
-How to Finally Start **Remembering Names**
-How to Have a Great Public Presentation
-How To Create Your Own **Unique Personality** in Business (and Everyday Life)
-Effective Networking
Direct link to Amazon Kindle Store: https://tinyurl.com/IanCommSkillsKindle

Paperback version on Createspace:

http://tinyurl.com/iancommunicationpaperback

Emotional Intelligence Training: A Practical Guide to Making Friends with Your Emotions and Raising Your EQ

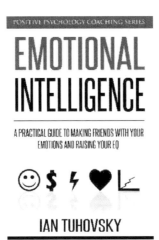

Do you believe your life would be healthier, happier and even better, if you had more practical strategies to regulate your own emotions?
Most people agree with that.
Or, more importantly:
Do you believe you'd be healthier and happier if everyone who you live with had the strategies to regulate their emotions?

...Right?

The truth is not too many people actually realize what EQ is really all about and what causes its popularity to grow constantly.

Scientific research conducted by many American and European universities prove that the **"common" intelligence responses account for less than 20% of our life achievements and successes, while the other over 80% depends on emotional intelligence.** To put it roughly: **either you are emotionally intelligent, or you're doomed to mediocrity, at best.**
As opposed to the popular image, emotionally intelligent people are not the ones who react impulsively and spontaneously, or who act lively and fiery in all types of social environments. Emotionally intelligent people are open to new experiences, can show feelings adequate to the situation, either good or bad, and find it easy to socialize with other people and establish new contacts. They handle stress well, say "no" easily, realistically assess the achievements of themselves or others and are not afraid of constructive criticism and taking calculated risks. **They are the people of success.** Unfortunately, this perfect model of an emotionally intelligent person is extremely rare in our modern times.

Sadly, nowadays, **the amount of emotional problems in the world is increasing at an alarming rate.** We are getting richer, but less and less happy. Depression, suicide, relationship breakdowns, loneliness of choice, fear of closeness, addictions—this is clear evidence that we are getting increasingly worse when it comes to dealing with our emotions.
Emotional intelligence is a SKILL, and can be learned through constant practice and training, just like riding a bike or swimming!

This book is stuffed with lots of effective exercises, helpful info and practical ideas.
Every chapter covers different areas of emotional intelligence and shows you, **step by step**, what exactly you can do to **develop your EQ** and become the **better version of yourself.**
I will show you how freeing yourself from the domination of left-sided brain thinking can contribute to your inner transformation—**the emotional revolution that will help you redefine who you are and what you really want from life!**

<u>**In This Book I'll Show You:**</u>

• What Is Emotional Intelligence and What Does EQ Consist of?
• How to **Observe and Express** Your Emotions
• How to **Release Negative Emotions** and **Empower the Positive Ones**
• How to Deal with Your **Internal Dialogues**
• How to **Deal with the Past**

- **How to Forgive** Yourself and How to Forgive Others
- How to Free Yourself from **Other People's Opinions and Judgments**
- What Are "Submodalities" and How Exactly You Can Use Them to **Empower Yourself** and **Get Rid of Stress**
- The Nine Things You Need to **Stop Doing to Yourself**
- How to Examine Your Thoughts
- **Internal Conflicts** Troubleshooting Technique
- The Lost Art of Asking Yourself the Right Questions and **Discovering Your True Self!**
- How to Create Rich Visualizations
- LOTS of practical exercises from the mighty arsenal of psychology, family therapy, NLP etc.
- **And many, many more!**

Direct Buy Link to Amazon Kindle Store:
https://tinyurl.com/IanEQTrainingKindle
Paperback version on Createspace: https://tinyurl.com/ianEQpaperback

Self-Discipline: Mental Toughness Mindset: Increase Your Grit and Focus to Become a Highly Productive (and Peaceful!) Person

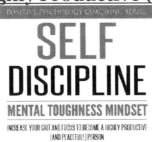

This Mindset and Exercises Will Help You Build Everlasting Self-Discipline and Unbeatable Willpower

Imagine that you have this rare kind of power that enables you to maintain iron resolve, crystal clarity, and everyday focus to gradually realize all of your dreams by consistently ticking one goal after another off your to-do list.

Way too often, people and their minds don't really play in one team.

Wouldn't that be profoundly life-changing to utilize that power to make the best partners with your brain?

This rare kind of power is a mindset. The way you think, the way you perceive and handle both the world around you and your inner reality, will ultimately determine the quality of your life.

A single shift in your perception can trigger meaningful results.

Life can be tough. Whenever we turn, there are obstacles blocking our way. Some are caused by our environment, and some by ourselves. Yet, we all know people who are able to overcome them consistently, and, simply speaking, become successful. And stay there!

What really elevates a regular Joe or Jane to superhero status is the laser-sharp focus, perseverance, and the ability to keep on going when everyone else would have quit.
I have, for a long time, studied the lives of the most disciplined people on this planet. In this book, you are going to learn their secrets.
No matter if your goals are financial, sport, relationship, or habit-changing oriented, this book covers it all.

Today, I want to share with you the science-based insights and field-tested methods that have helped me, my friends, and my clients change their lives and become real-life go-getters.

<u>**Here are some of the things you will learn from this book:**</u>

• **What the "positive thinking trap" means,** and how exactly should you use the power of positivity to actually help yourself instead of holding yourself back?
• What truly makes us happy and how does that relate to success? Is it money? Social position? Friends, family? Health? **No. There's actually something bigger, deeper, and much more fundamental behind our happiness.** You will be surprised to find out what the factor that ultimately drives us and keeps us going is, and this discovery can greatly improve your life.
• **Why our Western perception of both happiness and success are fundamentally wrong**, and how those misperceptions can kill your chances of succeeding?
• **Why relying on willpower and motivation is a very bad idea, and what to hold on to instead?** This is as important as using only the best gasoline in a top-grade sports car. Fill its engine with a moped fuel and keep the engine oil level low, and it won't get far. Your mind is this sports car engine. I will show you where to get this quality fuel from.
• **You will learn what the common denominator of the most successful and disciplined people on this planet is** – Navy SEALS and other special forces, Shaolin monks, top performing CEOs and Athletes, they, in fact, have a lot in common. I studied their lives for a long time, and now, it's time to share this knowledge with you.
• Why your entire life can be viewed as a piece of training, and **what are the rules of this training?**
• What the XX-th century Russian Nobel-Prize winner and long-forgotten genius Japanese psychotherapist **can teach you about the importance of your emotions and utilizing them correctly in your quest to becoming a self-disciplined and a peaceful person?**
• How modern science can help you **overcome temptation and empower your will,** and why following strict and inconvenient diets or regimens can actually help you achieve your goals in the end?
• How can you win by failing and **why giving up on some of your goals can actually be**

a good thing?
• How do we often become **our own biggest enemies** in achieving our goals and how to finally change it?
• How to **maintain** your success once you achieve it?

Direct Buy Link to Amazon Kindle Store:
http://tinyurl.com/IanMentalToughness
Paperback version on Createspace: http://tinyurl.com/IanMTPaperback

Mindfulness: The Most Effective Techniques: Connect With Your Inner Self to Reach Your Goals Easily and Peacefully

Mindfulness is not about complicated and otherworldly woo-woo spiritual practices. It doesn't require you to be a part of any religion or a movement.

What mindfulness is about is living a good life (that's quite practical, right?), and this book is all about deepening your awareness, **getting to know yourself**, and developing attitudes and mental habits that will make you not only a successful and effective person in life, but a happy and wise one as well.

If you have ever wondered what the mysterious words "mindfulness" means and why would anyone bother, you have just found your (detailed) answer!

This book will provide you with actionable steps and valuable information, all in plain English, so all of your doubts will be soon gone.

In my experience, **nothing has proven as simple and yet effective and powerful as the daily practice of mindfulness.**

It has helped me become more decisive, disciplined, focused, calm, and just a happier person.

I can come as far as to say that mindfulness has transformed me into a success.

Now, it's your turn.
There's nothing to lose, and so much to win!

The payoff is nothing less than transforming your life into its true potential.

What you will learn from this book:

-What exactly does the word "mindfulness" mean, and why should it become an important word in your dictionary?

-How taking **as little as five minutes a day** to clear your mind might result in steering your life towards great success and becoming a much more fulfilled person? ...and **how the heck can you "clear your mind" exactly?**

-What are the **most interesting, effective, and not well-known mindfulness techniques for success** that I personally use to stay on the track and achieve my goals daily while feeling calm and relaxed?

-**Where to start** and how to slowly get into mindfulness to avoid unnecessary confusion?

-What are the **scientifically proven profits** of a daily mindfulness practice?

-**How to develop the so-called "Nonjudgmental Awareness"** to win with discouragement and negative thoughts, **stick to the practice** and keep becoming a more focused, calm, disciplined, and peaceful person on a daily basis?

-What are **the most common problems** experienced by practitioners of mindfulness and meditation, and how to overcome them?

-How to meditate and **just how easy** can it be?

-What are **the most common mistakes** people keep doing when trying to get into meditation and mindfulness? How to avoid them?

-**Real life tested steps** to apply mindfulness to everyday life to become happier and much more successful person?

-What is the relation between mindfulness and life success? How to use mindfulness to become much more effective in your life and achieve your goals much easier?

-**What to do in life** when just about everything seems to go wrong?

-How to become a **more patient and disciplined person**?

Stop existing and start living.
Start changing your life for the better today.

<u>Buddhism: Beginner's Guide: Bring Peace and Happiness to Your Everyday Life</u>

Buddhism is one of the most practical and simple belief systems on this planet, and it has greatly helped me on my way to become a better person in every aspect possible. In this book I will show you what happened and how it was.

No matter if you are totally green when it comes to Buddha's teachings or maybe you have already heard something about them—this book will help you systematize your knowledge and will inspire you to learn more and to take steps to make your life positively better!

I invite you to take this beautiful journey into the graceful and meaningful world of Buddhism with me today!

About The Author

Author's blog: www.mindfulnessforsuccess.com
Author's Amazon profile: amazon.com/author/iantuhovsky
Instagram profile: https://instagram.com/mindfulnessforsuccess

Hi! I'm Ian...

...and I am interested in life. I am in the study of having an awesome and passionate life, which I believe is within the reach of practically everyone. I'm not a mentor or a guru. I'm just a guy who always knew there was more than we are told. I managed to turn my life around from way below my expectations to a really satisfying one, and now I want to share this fascinating journey with you so that you can do it, too.

I was born and raised somewhere in Eastern Europe, where Polar Bears eat people on the streets, we munch on snow instead of ice cream and there's only vodka instead of tap water, but since I make a living out of several different businesses, I move to a new country every couple of months. I also work as an HR consultant for various European companies.

I love self-development, traveling, recording music and providing value by helping others. I passionately read and write about social psychology, sociology, NLP, meditation, mindfulness, eastern philosophy, emotional intelligence, time management, communication skills and all of the topics related to conscious self-development and being the most awesome version of yourself.

Breathe. Relax. Feel that you're alive and smile. And never hesitate to contact me!

84396446R00090

Made in the USA
Lexington, KY
22 March 2018